Deliver

DELIVER

How to deliver software projects
using Agile ways of working

Peter Scheffer

Published by Peter Scheffer

First published in 2022 in Brisbane, Australia

Copyright © Peter Scheffer

www.peterscheffer.com

Brisbane, Queensland

All inquiries should be made to the author.

Edited by Jenny Magee

Designed, typeset and printed by BookPOD, Melbourne, Australia

ISBN: 978-0-6454897-0-5 (paperback)
ISBN: 978-0-6454897-1-2 (ebook)

Contents

Acknowledgements

A special thank you to Venky and Sean for proofreading, providing such valuable feedback and keeping me honest.

Thank you Paula, Mel and Karolina, for the inspiration and motivation to complete this book. Your feedback and encouragement convinced me to keep going.

Thanks to absent loved ones, Beth and Ken, who would be proud and know that their sacrifices were worth it. And Mal, who would have eclipsed my excitement at publishing my first book.

My thanks to the many other people who told me I should write; Adam, Brendan, Jeff, Brenda, Kate, Steve, and others I might have missed.

Thanks also to the many people who have taught and mentored me, and the great people I have worked with — particularly the FIAT crew at ANZ, the Digital Delivery team at UniSuper, and the Digital Technology Solutions team at Shell Energy.

♥

Preface

My reason for writing this book is simple — it's the book I wish I had when I was learning how to manage software delivery in Agile organisations. Much of the information captured in these pages is available elsewhere in books, on the internet, or in people's heads, but I needed a distilled, simplified and practical version of the content.

So I have created one for you and included only the most valuable and pragmatic information necessary to deliver projects successfully.

This book is for you if you are finding it difficult to apply Scrum or other Agile methods to the software development projects you are trying to deliver yourself or are deeply involved in. You understand the concepts of Scrum or Agile well enough, but there is a large gap between doing Scrum well and meeting the needs of your work colleagues and the expectations of your stakeholders. Their expectations limit you and your delivery team from delivering software using pure Scrum (or Agile more generally). A poll conducted by Atlassian discovered that ninety-two per cent of respondents run a customised version of Agile rather than 'by the book'.[1]

In these pages, I will teach you how to combine Scrum (or other Agile methods) with longer-term planning, risk and issue management, stakeholder management, progress reporting and improved estimation practices. I'll also explain some important activities to conduct before providing an estimate or kicking off your project.

These are the most common gaps where Scrum doesn't meet the needs of the organisation and project management practices.

Who am I to write this?

I have worked in most roles related to Agile software delivery. After seventeen years as a software engineer, I transitioned to work as a business analyst and did testing and iteration management. From there, I moved into a management role, overseeing a team of business analysts and iteration managers while taking on program management responsibilities. My next move was into a pure program management role, with portfolio management and team performance responsibilities. Having worked in many Agile work environments, I've seen many examples of good and bad practices.

I have led large, successful Agile transformations in two different organisations. These taught me the challenges of making Agile work. I also discovered the gaps between what Agile and Scrum training teaches and what is required to deliver a project successfully and meet stakeholder expectations.

The premise of this book is that you can ensure a better outcome for your project by conducting specific activities before and during development. These activities are designed to help you take a proactive approach by limiting or eliminating things that adversely impact delivery.

There are two approaches to delivery management. The proactive path seeks to identify problems before they become issues and implement activities to prevent problems from occurring. The benefit of proactive delivery management is that you greatly minimise the number and impact of issues, meaning increased control over project outcomes. This builds confidence and trust in your stakeholders, customers and team.

Reactive management means you respond to problems only when they have occurred, which usually resembles fire-fighting. The benefit is that you only commit effort and energy once a problem has been confirmed and needs rectifying. It can appear to require less effort than a proactive approach, but the reality is different. The effort to remediate a problem in software projects is almost always more costly than preventing the problem in the first place. Remember Benjamin Franklin's words; 'An ounce of prevention is worth a pound of cure' which curiously he said 'in order to remind the citizens of Philadelphia to remain vigilant about fire awareness and prevention'.[2]

The downside to reactive management is that it becomes an endless cycle once you start fire-fighting problems in a project. This is usually because quick solutions are sought to solve problems hastily and get the project back on track. Those solutions lead to further problems because they have not addressed the root cause and often create new problems. Reactive management robs you of the ability to think long-term, a skill that enables you to manage your project proactively. The danger is that your delivery team eventually becomes accustomed to constantly fighting fires and is frustrated and exhausted by the lack of forethought, planning and proper problem remediation. All of which can lead to team disengagement and staff departures.

This book is about longer-term planning and thinking and proactive delivery management to help you deliver successful software projects.

Introduction

Doing Scrum well can be extremely challenging, primarily because the way organisations are structured and operated creates limitations that prevent Scrum from working well. Many of those limitations are set by senior management and people with a lot of influence, meaning it is unlikely you can make changes easily or rapidly.

You will find that people compromise to apply Scrum as best they can. This book aims to bridge the gap between doing good Scrum and meeting the needs or limitations within your organisation. The book draws upon my experience in such environments and that of others who have faced similar circumstances.

It's helpful to know that this situation is fairly common. The primary reason for this is that many executives, managers and leaders are more familiar with traditional project and financial management practices. They apply those practices to projects within their accountability because that's their understanding of how to set and achieve project outcomes. By setting those expectations from the top, they enforce constraints that do not match Scrum practices.

Organisations can run Agile transformations to enable them to conduct Scrum practices better. However, those can still take years due to the amount of change required.

How this book is written

Words that are capitalised in the text represent the Agile-specific meaning of the word. An example is a User Story — which refers to a specific artefact used in Scrum to capture a user's requirements.

I will use the terms customer and user interchangeably. Your team might be building software for internal staff or external customers. Their software needs are much the same, however, your interactions with them and your definition of success may differ. For the purposes of this book, I've treated them the same — they are the end users who benefit from the software that your team is producing.

This book provides a range of options to address the challenges you might experience when delivering a project. While you do not need to apply everything taught in this book, I recommend testing each approach to learn the advantages and disadvantages and decide which ones best suit your situation and preferences.

A **cross-functional** team is one that includes people with complementary skills that (when combined) can build and release working software.

My assumptions about you

I'm assuming that you, the reader, are in a delivery type role or that you have been assigned delivery responsibilities. I also assume that you are working in an organisation with an intermediate knowledge of Agile and are trying to build software using Agile methods. Your organisation is likely running something resembling projects, and you are experiencing fairly typical project-style constraints. You face challenges with meeting stakeholders' expectations while trying to deliver the software in an Agile manner.

It's also likely that you have established long-standing cross-functional teams currently working in Scrum. If they are working in another flavour of Agile, then a lot of this information still applies, but you may need to adapt it to suit your circumstances.

Hopefully, you have some experience and training in Scrum and a good grasp of the concepts, but perhaps you do not know how to translate that into real-world activities that deliver successful outcomes.

This book assumes that most of your team's effort is software coding, testing and deploying, and not, for example, configuring a third-party software solution. The cost of writing a line of code is not negligible, meaning companies cannot ignore the outlay.

The cost of writing a line of code is not negligible, meaning the cost cannot be ignored by companies. How then can you avoid writing code that is unnecessary or wasteful?

Many companies mistakenly believe that code is cheap to produce and maintain, so they seek to solve many of their problems by implementing solutions in code without considering the costs. They treat the cost of producing code as zero or near-zero, and often do not compare the cost of producing working software with the expected value to be returned. This check is always essential as it tests the viability of the project. This book assumes that you are working in a medium- to large-sized enterprise that wishes to limit its software delivery costs.

Your team should aim to minimise the amount of code written and the number of re-writes and corrections they make. My philosophy is that it is far cheaper, easier and quicker to correct a mistake using pencil and paper (or a whiteboard) than to fix it in software. On paper, it takes minutes, whereas software takes days, weeks or even months.

This book will help you understand the customer's problem and the software design before writing a line of code to minimise mistakes. Most of the serious problems I have encountered are when teams have failed to understand the problem or design the solution well enough before building the software.

Who should read this?

If you are a Scrum Master, Iteration Manager, Product Owner, Delivery Lead, Delivery Manager, Project Manager, Program Manager, or in other delivery type roles, this book will provide actionable learnings that will help you successfully deliver software projects.

You'll find help here even if you have no prior delivery experience, but you'll need some real-world experience with Scrum or Agile.

What will we cover?

This book is about making software delivery work in an imperfect Agile environment, with constraints outside your control. It provides many tools, processes and techniques to lead to a better project outcome. It's up to you to choose which to apply and when.

We'll cover how to run project delivery while using Scrum, and how to marry Scrum with longer-term planning, reporting and stakeholder management. We'll discuss eliciting requirements from users, customers and stakeholders and converting the backlog into a plan or schedule for delivery.

The focus is on activities preceding project kick-off and planning and reporting activities through the delivery phase. We'll look at the challenges you will likely experience and proactive actions to prevent and manage them.

The first half of the book covers the activities that happen before starting delivery. These are more important than what happens during delivery because, if done correctly, they should make delivery easier and require less effort. This approach echoes Albert Einstein's famous words, 'If I had an hour to solve a problem, I'd spend fifty-five minutes thinking about the problem and five minutes thinking about solutions.'

In the second half of the book, we will explore how to create and manage a delivery plan, constantly revisiting progress and estimates to provide an up-to-date view of the project schedule.

This book covers how to run project delivery while using Scrum, and how to marry Scrum with longer-term planning, and stakeholder management and reporting.

CHAPTER ONE

Typical Project Challenges

Let's start with common project delivery challenges when using frameworks like Scrum. Sometimes the problems are to do with the teams' maturity to deliver in Agile, and sometimes those teams are limited by constraints outside their control. Either way, the pressures tend to be the same with project delivery.

Not getting requirements from your true customers

A common mistake is that the delivery team elicits the software requirements from people who don't represent the actual users — whether internal (staff) or external customers. This might occur at the outset of the project, where initial requirements are gathered or during review and feedback sessions. Either way, the users should be inspecting the working software and providing their requirements and feedback. The team must be able to engage these users because they will ultimately decide if the product is useful or not.

An associated mistake is that the delivery team works for months building the software before presenting the software for user review.

This can result in functionality that doesn't meet the users' needs or behave according to their requirements. The wasteful end result is that the delivery team has to rework a lot of already completed software.

Starting without knowing the full scale of work

Teams are often directed to start the work too early, without the opportunity first to conduct project Discovery. They are expected to learn the requirements and then design the solution along the way — without a view of the overarching goal or problem to be solved.

It's a common mistake, as, during delivery, the team learns that their solution design won't satisfy the users' needs or the project outcomes. They have to redesign the solution and rework a lot of the code that has already been written. The project scope increases dramatically as they learn what is needed from a user and a technical perspective.

The result is overrun in time and cost from original estimates. The project might be cut short to meet time and cost constraints, meaning the outcomes are not achieved, and the software doesn't satisfy the users' needs.

The learning here is that when there is a target deadline and budget for a project, a team can't simply start without forethought or planning and hope to meet the project constraints and outcomes. They need to do sufficient investigation to understand the entire body of work and how to achieve the expected outcomes, even if it's only a high-level understanding. Finding the right balance of upfront investigation versus learning through the delivery process is hard to manage and requires practice and experience.

The team needs to have designed a solution that can meet the overall needs of the users/customers and the project outcomes. There should be sufficient information to create the solution design and provide an educated estimate — especially if the team is accountable for meeting a deadline.

Not accounting for the complexity of the work

Sometimes a project is started without understanding the complexities inherent in the software solution. In many software projects, there are unknown complexities caused by any number of issues. These generally result in wildly incorrect time and cost estimates — and frustrated stakeholders and sponsors.

When projects run over schedule, pressure to finish quickly can mean shortcuts and sub-optimal project outcomes.

The learning here is that you must investigate what it will take to achieve the expected project outcomes. That means analysing the needs of users, customers and stakeholders. It also involves investigating any technical complexities in the solution design and accounting for them in the estimate or remediating technical complexity before providing an estimate.

Changing stakeholders part way through a project

In this scenario, a new, influential stakeholder might join a project that has been running for weeks or months, bringing new requirements or new constraints that weren't captured at the outset when an estimate was given. The result of their changes can mean unanticipated time and cost overruns. Without careful deliberation, those time and cost overruns can be blamed on the delivery team.

Agile principles tell us to *welcome changing requirements, even late in development.* We should be careful to accommodate new requirements or constraints with the view of the bigger picture, which is the product or business goal of the project and the work that has been completed and reviewed to date. If the new requirements do not align with the original goal, question whether the target has changed. If it has, ask what that means for meeting the initial goal and constraints of the project. If you and the team are expected to satisfy the changed goal, then you must revisit your estimates and delivery plan. In any case, if any new requirements create significant scope changes, then it is worthwhile estimating their impact and confirming acceptability with your stakeholders.

Other common challenges

A common challenge for delivery teams, stakeholders and sponsors is that it is unclear how much scope remains to complete a project and, therefore, how much more investment is required to reach the end. Progress reporting often simply states, 'We're almost there' until finally, someone in authority decides to stop the project. That means sponsors are expected to continue funding development without knowing how much ongoing funding or time is needed. In these circumstances, it is difficult to apply governance to a project, and senior stakeholders can get frustrated by Agile delivery methods.

Resistance to presenting working software to the customer and seeking their feedback means that the project team doesn't know if their software meets the users' needs. This is probably the most common and expensive risk in building software. One of Silicon Valley's most successful entrepreneurs, Steve Blank, explained in his post on the Lean Startup. '… too often, after months or even years of development, entrepreneurs learn the hard way that customers do not need or want most of the product's features.'[3]

Project failure rate

A study conducted by McKinsey found that 'On average, large IT projects run forty-five percent over budget and seven per cent over time, while delivering fifty-six percent less value than predicted. Software projects run the highest risk of cost and schedule overruns.'[4] They also found that 'The longer a project is scheduled to last, the more likely it is that it will run over time and budget, with every additional year spent on the project increasing cost overruns by fifteen percent.'[5]

Project complexity

I use the term *complexity* to encapsulate everything that makes a project challenging to deliver. It can represent many different aspects, such as the difficulty of solving real-world problems in code or creating software algorithms. There are challenges for the team in balancing the needs of many project stakeholders, understanding new technologies, legacy systems and integration. Most companies have existing software solutions that delivery teams must work with, and those legacy systems add a great deal of complexity to delivery.

Project complexity can also be valuable to your organisation because it can be a barrier to entry for your competitors. As Paul Graham put it, 'I can remember times when we were just exhausted after wrestling all day with some horrible technical problem. And I'd be delighted, because something that was hard for us would be impossible for our competitors.'[6] Of course, this only applies if the complex problem your team is solving is truly valuable to your customer.

Each organisation has a maturity and capability level that determines how much complexity it can manage before risking project failure. When teams first begin working in Scrum, they learn new ways of building software. They also manage the expectations of stakeholders who are often unfamiliar with Scrum. Your stakeholders may struggle with tracking delivery progress, iterative releases, adapting the product backlog, product owner accountabilities, and more. In this early stage, the delivery teams can face a greater project failure rate because the teams' delivery capability is immature.

Teams can also risk failure as the scale and complexity of projects increase. It is mainly due to the interdependent nature of projects and the need for increased collaboration, coordination and code management.

Helmsman International conducted a nine-year research study into the impact of complexity on project outcomes. They uncovered a specific and consistent scenario where the likelihood of project success plummets, calling it the Complexity Cliff.[7]

The following graph is re-created from their white paper and shows the correlation between complexity and performance. The dots represent the outcomes of historical projects, with a performance measure and complexity measure assigned to each project. As complexity increases (to the right of the graph), the likelihood of success drops below fifty per cent. The trend line shows project performance falling off the cliff.

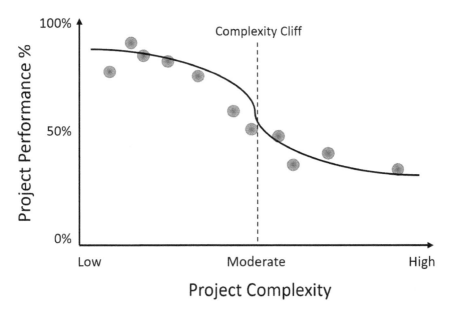

Figure 1: Representation of the Complexity Cliff

This graph shows that projects on the right side of the Complexity Cliff require greater delivery maturity than the current organisational capability. Those on the left are within the host organisation's ability to deliver successfully.

That tells us that for the organisation to have successful projects, it can either only conduct simple (or less complex) projects or increase the capability of the organisation to deliver more complex projects.

CHAPTER TWO

Starting with Scrum

I'm assuming that you have already started moving to Agile ways of working by beginning with Scrum. Scrum is well-known, has been used for many years, and has a great deal of training and coaching available to get you started.

Scrum tends to be the first framework that teams apply, which makes sense as it is one of the most well-documented. It details the role and accountability of team members and explains the activities needed to collaborate, complete work and adapt the solution.

That doesn't make it easy, though. Shifting from Waterfall to Scrum is one of the most transformational and challenging changes your team can undertake, and getting it right can take a lot of trial and error.

Scrum is difficult to run in a company that maintains traditional views of project management and financial management. It can require organisational change to fully succeed.

When making the transition, you may find that some areas (roles and responsibilities, estimation) may not make sense. There is strong temptation to map old roles and methods onto new ones, and often the move to Scrum fails because people apply the labels but don't change their ways of working.

Scrum changes more than just how the delivery team operates. It also shapes how the team engages with customers and how requirements are gathered. It changes the order of delivery and the demands upon the people around the software team. It affects what working software the end user will see and when they will see it. Other aspects, including project capitalisation, how team members are allocated, and how deadlines are met are also impacted. Applying Scrum successfully requires buy-in from your stakeholders, the management team and customers.

You will likely have found that true Scrum is very difficult to apply in an established delivery team or corporate environment. Many factors make this so, and some will be beyond your control to change.

Within a corporate environment, there are expectations according to the constraints set by your stakeholders. These usually mean delivering on time and on budget, or something similar. Scrum doesn't provide you with the means to achieve this, so there is a gap.

Many senior stakeholders and managers believe that the team will deliver faster or increase their throughput by applying the Scrum framework. They perceive Scrum as a solution to particular delivery problems. However, Scrum is designed to make customer satisfaction the highest priority, not increase throughput or deliver faster or meet a deadline. Its purpose is to give working software to customers sooner and more frequently. That is not the same as working faster.

In this book, I want to fill the gap between what Scrum teaches you and the needs of your stakeholders. It won't provide everything you need to make Scrum work within your organisation, but it will enable you to deliver software well while still applying Agile ways of working.

The primary characteristics of projects are that your stakeholders assume a roughly fixed or known set of scope requirements, and you may be constrained by time and cost. That means that a pure Scrum approach will not give your stakeholders what they expect.

CHAPTER THREE

Discovery

We must start any reasonable-sized project by understanding the constraints and the perceived scope of work to be delivered. We call this period of understanding, *Discovery*, and it improves your likelihood of successfully delivering a significant project.

Discovery prework can be conducted as a single workshop or spread over days or weeks. If you only apply Scrum to delivering a project, there will be plenty of gaps, and Discovery fills many of those.

Discovery helps teams rapidly understand the problem space and potential solutions for the software by creating and discussing low-cost artefacts. Through this understanding, the team minimises the risks and challenges of delivery.

An **artefact** is any kind of document, diagram, working prototype, proof of concept, or other item that helps people to understand the problem and the proposed solution.

The value of Discovery is in minimising corrections and misunderstandings for things that are unlikely to change once the project is underway, which includes things like the high-level solution design and high-level customer needs. It is not designed to provide a fixed set of requirements, but rather it's the starting point for deeper analysis and requirements elicitation.

Discovery provides a sufficient level of breadth and depth so that a team can comprehend the extensive body of work ahead before writing the first line of code. The team should have sufficient understanding to create a solution design that answers the most difficult questions in a few diagrams. That could be an architecture diagram, a process flow, or a user interface design — whatever best enables them to answer questions about their solution.

Discovery is not intended to be as in-depth as traditional Waterfall business analysis, software design and technical specification. Agile principles tell us that *the best architectures, requirements, and designs emerge from self-organising teams.* The design I am describing provides an initial solution to start working with — one that considers the broad needs of the customer, stakeholders and project outcomes.

Discovery provides your team with a high-level view of the problem space and the possible solution space.

Discovery provides your team with a high-level view of the problem and possible solution space. This allows them to start designing a solution that meets the needs of the overall problem or product goal.

It becomes more important when teams deal with complex problems, interdependent projects, legacy systems, or where the solution design must fit with existing software.

The level of Discovery needed depends upon the size and complexity of the project, and the experience of the team members doing the work. It also relies on the willingness and ease of all people involved to agree on a range of decisions. As teams and stakeholders become more experienced, the Discovery phase can become shorter.

Watch for the Project Lisbon boxes throughout the book. These describe a hypothetical project to explain some concepts. We start with a Project Brief that gives a sense of what the project is about.

Project Lisbon

You have been assigned to oversee a new business initiative for a customer-facing product. The Project Brief is fairly simple and straightforward. 'Build an event-booking portal. Customers can search, select and book events listed on the site.'

Discovery encompasses the end user's needs, the needs of important stakeholders and sponsors, and the team delivering the software. Be cautious when taking this approach to delivery, as it may give stakeholders and sponsors a belief that everything has been agreed upon and decided up front and that, as a result, the estimates, budget and timeline are all fixed and well-known. This goes against one of Agile's stated values, *responding to change over following a plan*. It's important to set clear expectations that things will change throughout delivery, and that allowing for change is a desirable characteristic because it creates better software outcomes for customers.

At a high level, the Discovery process looks like the diagram in figure 2. In reality, it may not be so linear and some steps may be combined or repeated.

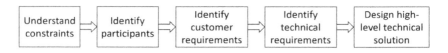

Figure 2: High-level Discovery process

We start by understanding what constraints apply to the delivery team, the software and the project. These place limitations on the scope of work, possible solutions, and how to implement the solution. Knowing the constraints in advance means the team avoids wasting time proposing and experimenting with designs that do not meet them.

The next step is to identify all the people relevant to the delivery of the project and its outcomes. This avoids finding requirements and expectations late in the project that can cause additional work or rework, all of which impact delivery schedules.

It's at this point where the usual project constraints and Scrum disagree. Scrum wants to allow for changes, even late ones, whereas project stakeholders typically want some surety that the project will not significantly exceed initial estimates. I will explain how to enable flexible timelines and scope of work in Chapter Five, Estimation and Capacity. For now, we want to know what expectations and limitations our stakeholders place upon the project before starting.

Once you have collated the list of constraints and stakeholders, you can book the first workshop with the stakeholders and your team to begin understanding the requirements and expectations of the project. We will explore this process in the Scope of work.

The benefit of doing Discovery upfront is that while you and your team explore the problem space and propose solutions, any mistakes are made using pencil and paper (or whiteboard, or sticky notes, etc.), so the cost of correcting them is negligible. Not only that, but you are utilising the wisdom of the crowd because you have everyone in the room who might know something valuable about the project, and their knowledge can help you and your team quickly navigate potential obstacles.

The mistakes you might correct could be technical solutions or software design that is unsuitable from the perspective of the overall customer problem. Or it may be that the customer problem has not been fully understood correctly, or the solution doesn't satisfy systems integration. Many of these mistakes result in extensive rewrites of completed functionality. Capturing and fixing them in Discovery saves time, money and frustration.

When engineers solve a problem alone, they only have their personal knowledge to call upon. With a team of experts across all aspects of the business domain, they have far greater ability to produce an excellent solution. Never underestimate the power of having all those important people hear each other's proposals, challenges, and solutions and then respond in real-time with their thoughts and opinions.

Understand constraints

If you work in an established delivery team or an established organisation, conditions will likely apply to your software delivery and the solution. It is much better to know these before starting the work or providing an estimate than to discover them partway through delivering a software product or project. Your stakeholders and sponsors assume that you are aware and have factored them into your delivery schedule, and you demonstrate your capability by showing that you have done so.

You shouldn't need to understand the constraints in detail, but you must ensure that they have been accommodated in the solution design, the planning and the estimation. That generally means that you need to get the delivery team to collaborate with everyone and anyone needed to understand them.

These conditions might be familiar to existing team members but entirely unknown to new people. All your team must understand them as they may create overheads that impact the effort and timelines of the work.

Constraints can be beneficial because they limit the options available and encourage the team to innovate around them.

One last comment on constraints before exploring them in detail. Even though it may seem counter-intuitive, constraints can be beneficial to software development teams. For example, without time limitations, projects can suffer from constant re-designing as teams keep reimagining better ways to implement the solution. They can also devise more elaborate technical solutions than are necessary. However, the benefit for the customer or end user is negligible between one technical solution and another, so the engineers are not adding additional value. Adding value is at the heart of Agile delivery, so creating that focus for the team is essential.

Steve Jobs famously threw an early version of the iPod into an aquarium. When bubbles floated out, he snapped, 'Those are air bubbles. That means there's space in there. Make it smaller.'[8] In doing so, he inadvertently set a constraint for the team and forced them to innovate to reduce the size of the iPod. While early versions were 19.8mm thick, now, years later, they are 6.1mm thick, so the constraint had the desired effect.

Let's explore the kinds of constraints you are likely to experience. Then you can ask the right questions to discover which you need to account for.

Architecture

Often, an approved architecture will apply to the technical solution design. It describes a broad range of factors that need to be considered, including system integration, data design, database architecture, networking, event handling, services, etc. There should be a person representing the prescribed architecture with whom your team can consult to discuss and understand the constraints on the solution design.

Technology

This might be covered by architecture, but if specific technologies are required, this too is a constraint. You will find that delivery teams and IT groups prefer to maintain consistent technology stacks to reduce the complexity and breadth of skillsets needed to support IT systems.

Check that your delivery team has the skills and experience required to work with the technology. Once the solution design has been developed, ensure that the chosen technology doesn't prevent the team from achieving the project outcome. Sometimes a chosen technology can't meet the solution's needs. That means teams must find workarounds or rework the solution — both of which are usually costly.

Engineering and testing practices

Often an established organisation will have prescribed engineering and testing practices. These practices ensure quality standards are met, and that code can be better managed throughout its lifecycle. These practices can cover various aspects, such as coding standards and styles, branching and merging, code review, continuous integration and deployment, environment and data management. All of which can add overhead to the project schedule.

Documentation practices

Some organisations have documentation requirements that may involve the delivery team. These are often overlooked as they are not considered part of delivering working software. If not factored into the estimate and schedule, they can come as a surprise.

System landscape

When working in an established organisation, the delivery team and the solution design often operate within the constraints of existing software systems. They may need to integrate with them, build on top of them, or even need to refactor certain parts. This can add significant effort to the workload and uncertainty to the schedule and delivery plan. If the delivery team is unfamiliar with the existing systems, it may take considerable time to understand the systems, work with the existing code and make changes. It is also possible that team members do not have the required skills to modify the legacy system.

Approvals

Approvals can surprise teams and impact delivery schedules. Existing organisations often have layers of processes and checkpoints that require some kind of formal approval to proceed. These can cause significant delays, impacting the team's ability to continue working. A single-person dependency or many approval steps throughout the delivery process can generate unexpected increases to delivery schedules throughout the project.

Resources

The delivery team requires a range of resources to do their job, and often there are unexpected resource issues. These could include licensing and software necessary for team members to do their job, hardware such as a laptop or development environment, access permissions to buildings or databases, and experts with particular knowledge or skills. Anything that prevents the team from doing their day job can cause delays. If even one person is delayed, the domino effect causes setbacks to other team members and the schedule.

Some teams adopt the concept of *sprint zero* — a period set aside at the start of a project to ensure that all team members have what they need to start working. You can incorporate these activities into the Discovery phase.

Third-party vendor

Dependency on an external vendor can be one of the greatest challenges to manage as you may have little influence or control over their schedule and delivery management. They may not work in the same iterative delivery method as your team. If they choose to deliver their fully functional solution at the very end of your delivery schedule, you could find it doesn't integrate properly, has defects, or doesn't meet the requirements. All this can add a great deal of risk to your delivery.

Integration

Established organisations often have legacy software systems that have either been built internally or purchased from external vendors. These systems are critical for the business because they hold essential data or perform vital processing or communication workflows. Your project may need to integrate with these systems.

This acts as a constraint because integrating with these systems is the only way to access the needed data or perform the necessary processing. It can present considerable risk and complexity because there's usually limited information on how to integrate with the systems, or they simply don't provide the integration you need. This limitation is worth exploring in-depth before providing an estimate, because it represents a significant chance of getting the estimate wrong.

During the Discovery process, I strongly recommend that the team focuses on integration challenges and efforts, pulling together whatever information is available. Where the documentation is insufficient or a third-party vendor needs to be engaged, allocate significant time to understand the technical side of integration with the relevant systems.

Budget

Your project might have a sponsor within the organisation whose job is to ensure that you have controlled costs to meet an agreed budget. Budget constraints can be challenging to deal with and are usually the greatest influence preventing true Agile (iterative) delivery because they are deemed to be fixed.

The ideal situation is to have a flexible budget that adapts to the needs and feedback from the customer as the team builds the software. However, this is rarely the case in traditional project management. A sponsor or financial controller is often assigned to oversee costs tracked against the budget to ensure that the budget is not exceeded. I will cover estimation and methods to manage expectations and adaptability in Chapter Five: Estimation and Capacity.

Time

As with budget constraints, someone usually oversees progress against the delivery schedule to ensure it is completed on time. Again, there are ways to manage expectations and provide adaptability that I will cover later in the book.

Scope of work

Start the Discovery workshops by focusing on a high-level understanding of what success looks like and clarity of your users'/customers' and stakeholders' expectations. In further workshops, you can refine that understanding and design a technical solution that meets those needs.

A predetermined set of features or functionality is expected to be delivered in most software projects. The scope may not be clearly known, but there is some expectation from stakeholders and/or end users that the software satisfies particular needs or problems.

Project Lisbon

Your stakeholders assume that the working software will have the minimum set of features available so that the product can go to market and satisfy the basic needs of customers who want to be able to book events.

Nobody has yet articulated what those features are — or what they should be. Your stakeholders will make assumptions from their own experience using booking websites and mobile applications. They each have different ideas of what 'good' looks like. They expect your team to design a good solution.

You will need to discover this minimum set of features.

Agile provides better results because the solution adapts to the needs of the customer through regular inspection and feedback.

That doesn't mean you should capture a specific set of detailed requirements upfront in the traditional Waterfall method, however, you need an understanding of the high-level features and functionality expected. You should deeply understand the system needs. 'Scope of work' refers to the high-level scope of features and system needs required to deliver the project outcome successfully.

Agile delivers superior software outcomes because end users, customers, and stakeholders get to inspect the software at regular intervals throughout the software development process. They can then provide feedback and change any aspect of the software to meet their needs better. That means the requirements are emergent as the result of inspecting working software.

Requirements gathered through inspection and delivered via adaption give far better software outcomes than traditional Waterfall methods. That is because they are more accurate and relevant to the software solution and the users' needs. We will explore this in greater detail later. For now, understand that the scope of work will continue to grow as the team learns the customers' needs.

One of the challenges delivery teams face is that they begin coding the solution too soon, without fully understanding the scope of work at a high level. They often realise part way through delivery that their technical solution will not meet the overall business and customer needs, and they will have to change the design. The resulting rework impacts delivery schedules.

Ideally, the team has sufficient time in advance to understand the full scope of the problem they are solving and create a high-level solution that encompasses all the high-level requirements to deliver a good outcome.

The following are some well-known methods to explore the problem space and avoid solutioning until the problem space is understood and the scope of the problem is confirmed. The goal here is to stay down the ladder of inference, not jump to conclusions about which problem needs to be solved. Another common issue within software teams is the assumption that they understand the users' problems and needs. They then begin building too early, only to find that they have incorrectly understood them, resulting in further rework.

The following techniques can be used at any time while understanding requirements, including during User Story elaboration and refinement.

Empathise

Tools and methods are available to help you empathise with customers and end users. These allow you to understand the problems they face in the real world and help you to target specific issues that you can solve with the software. The most well-known method is Ideo's Design Thinking, which encompasses different techniques that you can apply depending upon the circumstances. '[Design Thinking] encourages organizations to focus on the people they're creating for, which leads to better products, services, and internal processes. When you sit down to create a solution for a business need, the first question should always be, "What's the human need behind it?"'[9]

The benefit of empathising is that you understand the users' actual needs early, ideally by observing them within their work environment. This removes much of the assumption and interpretation from requirements gathering. Empathising means putting yourself in the users' shoes to understand what work they are trying to do, what problems they are trying to solve, and what pressures they face that can make software difficult to use.

Project Lisbon

The customers who will use your software product will likely already be booking events, perhaps with other companies and their existing websites and mobile apps. These customers can share their experiences to help you design a good solution.

To empathise, you might interview or survey them to ask about their experiences with event booking tools; Which tools do they like and why? What problems do they encounter regularly? How would they design a tool to make booking events easier? What

---

problems or activities are they trying to complete when booking an event?

To get more valuable data and information, you might ask to observe them using some of their preferred tools. You will see the kinds of pain they experience and some of the wins they get.

If they don't use online tools, then ask how they currently complete tasks and activities associated with the product you are building.

Five Whys

We are often presented with requirements from users, customers and stakeholders that represent what those people strongly believe are the problems that need to be solved.

The reality is more likely that those needs represent the symptoms and not the real, underlying problem. That means that if we solution according to the requirements we are first given, we haven't solved the underlying issue, and it will continue to present itself in different ways.

Requirements given by users often need further analysis to determine the root cause of underlying problems and desires.

There is a simple technique for getting to the root of a problem called the Five Whys.[10] The goal here is to challenge the assumptions and understanding of the person giving you the requirements to see if you can uncover the true cause of the problem they are describing.

An example might be a customer who explains, 'Whenever I am on this screen and submit the form, it takes forever. I just want to go to the next screen. I need a big button that says "Go to next screen" which does exactly that'.

The underlying cause might be that the software is doing some kind of processing that the user is unaware of, which takes a long time, delaying the loading of the next screen. The symptom is the long delay experienced by the user, but the cause is the thing that needs to be resolved. Asking the Five Whys of the user and the delivery team should help identify the actual cause of the delay.

It might go like this:

User: 'I need a button to take me to the next screen.'

Product Owner: 'Why?'

User: 'Because the software stops responding when I submit the form. It does nothing for a long time.'

Product Owner: 'Why does it take a long time and not respond?'

User: 'I don't know why.'

Product Owner: 'Does anyone on the team know why?'

Team member: 'Yes, because a service is processing a large amount of data before showing the results on the next screen.'

Product Owner: 'Why does the software wait until that point to process all the data at once?'

Team member: 'The software was built that way originally.'

Product Owner: 'Why was it built that way?'

Team member: 'It was a constraint of how the software library did state management five years ago. They have improved the library since then, but our code hasn't been changed to take advantage of the improvements.'

Product Owner: 'Okay, let's investigate how to speed it up.'

This should result in creating a backlog item designed to address the root cause of the problem that the user is experiencing. It might also mean that adding a 'button to go to the next screen' is unnecessary.

Business process mapping

Many businesses automate their business processes to improve their service delivery or back-office management. It is useful to model the business process in a document and discuss and confirm the team's understanding.

Often this visual process can be used to identify improvements by looking for blockages and issues that delay or confuse the process. Sometimes it helps to map the *as is* business process and the *to be* business process. This allows the team to understand what process changes need to be implemented and provides them with the opportunity to ask important questions. Having a visual representation of the business process can help the team identify the work that is needed.

The team can be asked to share their views on what is needed to build the software solution based on their understanding of the business process.

Business processes can be much harder to change once implemented in software, so make sure they're efficient first.

Any visual artefact that can help the team articulate what work is required to deliver the solution is beneficial.

We must confirm that the design represents the best possible implementation of the business process, as the user's or stakeholder's process requirements are often accepted as a given. If nobody asks how to improve the process, the software could make a bad or inefficient business process very difficult to change. It is easier to change a process when it is manual than when it has been implemented in code. And better to design the solution on paper and confirm that it is efficient.

Project Lisbon

Here is a greatly simplified example of a business process map for our event booking website. It shows the three key actors of the process as three separate swimlanes: the Customer, Your Company and Event Organiser. Actors can be humans or software. Each swimlane is a timeline representing the order of activities, from left to right. The rounded boxes represent activities or tasks that need to be completed by someone or by the software. The dotted lines indicate interactions between the actors. The letter icon represents a notification sent in whatever suitable format.

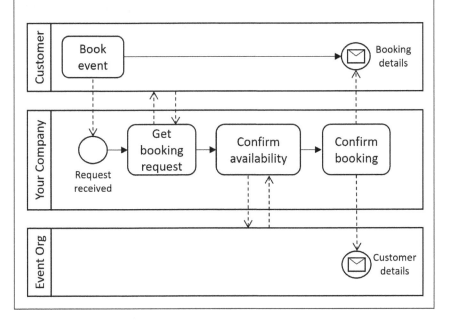

User experience design

User experience design (commonly 'UX') helps explain the interaction between the user and the software. UX can provide descriptions of screen elements, screen flow, user interactions, colours and their meanings and specific language usage. This is very useful for helping the team identify what work needs to be completed to deliver the working software.

Users generally find it easier to discuss screen designs and screen flow, to clarify and confirm requirements. Most users think about screen elements and user interfaces when describing software and their needs, so having a visual representation can elicit requirements quickly.

It shouldn't matter whether you use high fidelity (very detailed) screen designs or simple wireframes, assuming that the screen elements obviously represent how the user interacts with them. Wireframes are the easiest to change rapidly.

Project Lisbon

Here is an example of a wireframe. It presents us with the rough layout of a user interface for a single screen or web page. It shows the interactive elements and gives an idea of what function each screen element performs. A screen flow would include wireframes for multiple screens and show how users navigate between them to complete their tasks and objectives. This level of detail should be sufficient for users to understand how to complete their tasks and activities and confirm that the functionality meets their needs.

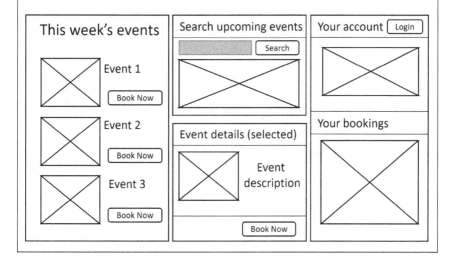

When the designer walks through the designs and answers questions, they receive feedback, and the user has a clear understanding of how the interface is designed to be operated.

Other useful artefacts

Many other standard solution design documents can be created to help the delivery team understand the scope of work, for example, high-level architecture design, data flow diagram, event or sequence diagram, component diagram, and state machine diagram.

Some of these artefacts can only be created after the technical solution is known. Each helps draw the picture for the delivery team to understand what work needs to be completed and what challenges might be faced. The team's ability to define the technical requirements of the software often depends upon having this level of detail.

These diagrams can become the 'cheat sheet' for new team members to learn rapidly what and how functionality is being built. They are maps that show an engineer or tester how to navigate the source code or user interface.

Not all of these artefacts are needed, and the delivery team should become familiar enough to know which will provide the most clarity.

Define success measures

Defining the initiative's success is essential to help the delivery team have a goal and understand the needs of the various users and stakeholders. Your stakeholders can be anyone who influences the success of the project. Consider people such as managers who oversee staff who may use the software (if it is internal) or people within the organisation who are impacted by changes to business processes or their software as a by-product of your project. You might involve project sponsors or people who have a vested interest in tracking the project costs. Others might be people

Success measures help the team understand the vision for the product, and to build a solution with the end in mind.

who depend on your software being completed (perhaps for their own project) or those responsible for the software quality, such as practice managers.

You should be able to consult a broad range of end users and stakeholders to determine what a successful outcome means for them. This will produce a long list that often resembles outcome-based requirements rather than functional requirements.

An example might be 'I no longer have to upload a large number of files' or 'I no longer have to wait five minutes for files to load'.

These can also be business-oriented success measures, such as 'Customers increase their adoption of the new interface by twenty-five per cent'. All of these requirements help to define the work to be done.

If you can apply measures to some of these outcome-based requirements, then you have a good starting position for understanding the needs of the software and can empirically prove that it has achieved its goal once it is complete.

Requirements elicitation

Your goal is to compile a list of unique features and functions that the software is expected to provide. It often helps your users and stakeholders to formulate their needs by asking them to phrase their requirements with the words 'I have the ability to …'.

Your team can do this as well when trying to define the needs of the software when studying the solution design documents (covered above). If there is something that the software needs to do and they are struggling to describe it as a requirement, then ask them to explain it using the words 'It needs to have the ability to …'.

This exercise helps them think about the problem space and possible solutions without going into the technicalities of how the solution needs to look and act. People with technical skills tend to want to think of problems in terms of technical solutions, but this can blur the discussion and make it hard to crystalise the problem.

Sometimes the team can be too heavily influenced by users who describe the look and behaviour of the software. The solution design should be managed by the team and decided separately from capturing the requirements.

A good example is a user who is asked to describe their requirements but talks instead about the solution design (e.g., 'When I click the button'). It's okay for users to use this language, but your team should be careful not to limit solution design by capturing these descriptions as requirements.

Instead, use more general language like 'When the user submits the form' or 'moves to the next step in the process' or 'selects from the available options'. The software designer has the greatest flexibility by taking this approach and may decide not to use a button or a click behaviour.

In this early stage of exploring the problem space, your team members must remain solution-agnostic, meaning they should not be discussing and thinking about how to implement the requirements in software yet. Remember that the goal at this stage is to 'stay down the ladder of inference', so try to avoid making technical decisions that (once decided) are very hard to undo and limit alternative options.

Impact mapping

There is a technique for identifying customer and business goals that indicates what work needs to be completed. You can apply this at the start of Discovery and continue to use it to elicit requirements and product goals throughout the development process.

The idea is to list four categories; Goal, Actor, Impact, and Deliverable, which represent Why, Who, How, and What is needed to achieve the goal. Beneath those headings, your stakeholders, users and team will collaborate to fill in these categories. See the diagram in figure 3 for an example.

Impact mapping starts with what impact the software will have, and works backwards to learn what deliverables are needed.

Define your goal using SMART, a *Specific, Measurable, Achievable, Relevant (or Realistic)* and *Time-bound* outcome.

Next, identify the Actors who can impact the goal, including those outside your organisation who may be contributors, including the customer.

The Impact represents the observable changes that contribute toward the goal, usually as a measurable outcome.

Finally, identify Deliverables — those things the team will need to build to achieve those impacts. They should be easily identifiable, and if not, your users and stakeholders should help you identify them.

An excellent book that explains this approach is *Impact Mapping: Making a Big Impact with Software Products and Projects* by Gojko Adzic.[11]

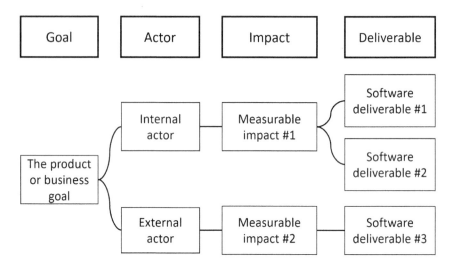

Figure 3: Impact mapping and how it identifies deliverables

Note that there is only one goal on the left-hand side, but there can be any number of actors, impacts and deliverables. You might want to limit how many you add to one diagram to manage the discussion better.

The deliverables on the right-hand side might be too high level and need to be broken down into more specific Epics and User Stories.

Project Lisbon

Imagine that the event booking website has already been operating, and the company has event managers whose responsibility is to increase sales through repeat custom. We can see the impact map as follows. The business goal is on the left, and we arrive at the deliverables on the right through analysis. Note that the customer takes a role in achieving the business goal. This is an important consideration because it helps us realise that we need to satisfy the customer's needs to achieve our goal.

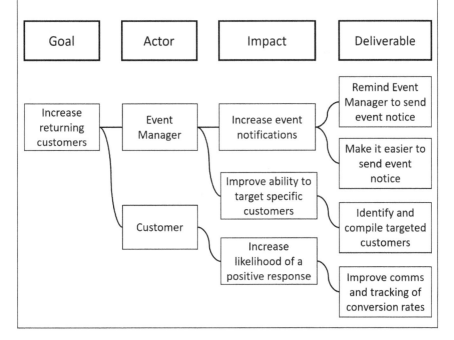

Measuring outcomes

Following the previous example, once you identify a measurable goal, use the goal and impacts to determine measurable outcomes.

There are two different types of measurements to consider, categorised into *leading* indicators and *lagging* indicators.

Measuring outcomes is the only reliable way of knowing that you have delivered value.

Leading indicators are things that we can measure from the moment the software is used. Lagging indicators take time to change and may not be measurable immediately. They generally confirm a trend, whereas leading indicators anticipate a successful outcome if particular benchmarks are met.

The following diagram (figure 4) continues from the previous Impact Mapping example, using target outcomes that the organisation hopes to achieve. These can be used to define the Product Goals or contribute towards the Product Goals and need to be confirmed by the Product Owner.

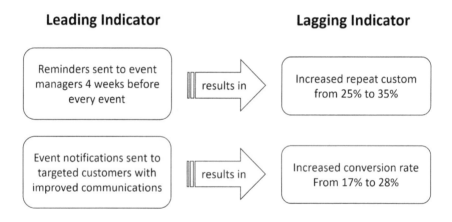

Figure 4: Leading and lagging indicators

Types of outcomes to measure

It's valuable to understand that you can measure quantitative *and* qualitative outcomes. Directly observing quantitative outcomes determines the results. Qualitative outcomes are subjective and experiential (can only be described by someone who experiences them) and are measured through user surveys and interviews. Compare the examples in figure 5.

Quantitative Factors		Qualitative Factors	
Keywords	Examples	Keywords	Examples
Faster, cheaper	Faster screen loading time	Better	Better user experience
More, less	More weekly registrations	Private	Enhanced personal privacy
Increase, decrease	Decrease in user errors	Easier	Easier to input data
Can, cannot	Can access their own private data	Improve	Improved screen flow
Don't have to	Do not have to print forms any more	Enjoyable	Enjoyable screen design
Compliant	Complies with specific government regulations	Transparent	Easier to interpret
Consistent	Standardised data representation	Richer	Elaborate information

Figure 5: Examples of measurable outcomes

Technical requirements

Your delivery team should be able to identify the technical requirements as part of the Discovery process. This involves examining the artefacts, thinking about the needs of the software and adding their own ideas about the problems to be solved or functional requirements that will add value.

For example, when a team member hears that a list of items is sorted in a unique manner, they will need to find a *way* to do the sorting. Another example might be that the interface needs to display data from two different data sources, so the team captures the need to figure out how to query and retrieve the data and merge it.

Throughout the Discovery process, prompt the team by asking questions, such as, 'Do you know how we can do that?' or 'How might we do that?' or 'Is that a problem we will need to solve?'

This activity might be better to complete without other stakeholders and users present, as it can be lengthy and tedious for them. You and your team will know who to invite to each workshop.

Solutioning

Once you have gathered the broad set of high-level software requirements, it is time to begin designing the solution. You should now have an agreed set of constraints and technical requirements that will reduce possible solution designs.

Narrowing the options simplifies the process of designing the solution. You can also descope items you've agreed are not required. We will discuss how to do this in the Process section.

The team can now start the process of designing the solution. There is always a danger of narrowing the solution options too rapidly or being heavily influenced by a single person or suggestion. Once an approach has been suggested and adopted, it is difficult for the team to broaden their thinking again and explore other solution options. That could mean that they end up with a suboptimal choice.

One technique can help the team avoid this when creating the design. The idea is to brainstorm the possible range of options by having everyone answer the question 'How might we?' for each decision point. The team can explore all possibilities by listing each option and avoiding selecting one too early. Once the full range is available, the team can choose the optimal one.

An example might be, 'The user has a requirement that they can upload all of the files at once. *How might we* create the ability to upload all files at once?' What follows should be the team brainstorming many alternative solutions.

At this stage, the team members still haven't written any code — they are simply explaining how they might create an appropriate solution. They could use diagrams or whiteboard designs to help explain their approach. The idea is to avoid investing too much time or effort right now, as any requirement or proposed solution could be cancelled or rejected at any time.

Resolving technical unknowns

When moving to Agile ways of working and utilising Discovery, you may find that the team has been unable to address all the unknowns before starting delivery, adding uncertainty to the schedule.

A common method for addressing technical unknowns and complexity is a Spike, which can occur at any point during the software development process. It is an opportunity for the team to conduct rapid experiments, usually through writing code, to address perceived problems in their solution design and their understanding of new

A Spike is a way for a team to rapidly research solutions to give them confidence that they are able to solve a difficult or unfamiliar problem.

technology or the business domain. The delivery team can run Spikes in the Discovery phase to gain confidence in the proposed solution. They can also build a Proof of Concept (or POC) that might be more detailed and functional than a Spike. A Proof of Concept is working software that solves a specific problem, and can then become part of the completed software. The purpose of conducting a POC is to prove that the team knows how to solve a technical challenge.

Identify participants

Ahead of Discovery, it is worth determining who is involved in your project and their level of involvement. This is especially important if it is a new team or project, or your team has changed their roles or ways of working. Look beyond the delivery team to who else should be involved and understand what their involvement looks like. Use the diagram in figure 6 to discuss and decide which workshops they should participate in.

Stakeholder map

A stakeholder map can be a simple diagram or table showing the names and roles of people involved in delivering the software, including stakeholders and sponsors. It can describe which meetings or ceremonies they are expected to participate in. It can show who the delivery team members depend upon to make decisions. It can show who has what interest in the outcome of the project. And it helps newcomers understand who their stakeholders are.

The following example shows how to map names and roles, so everyone understands their relationship and involvement in the project.

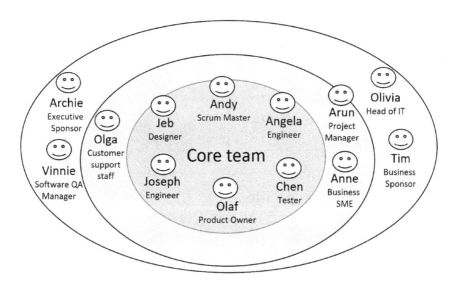

Figure 6: Stakeholder onion map

The *Core team* does the day-to-day activities that deliver the project. People outside that circle are consulted or engaged only when needed. People in the circle closest to the core team have more engagement with the team than those furthest.

Use a different stakeholder map to document each person's interest in the project so you know who to engage and when — based on their interest level and amount of influence.

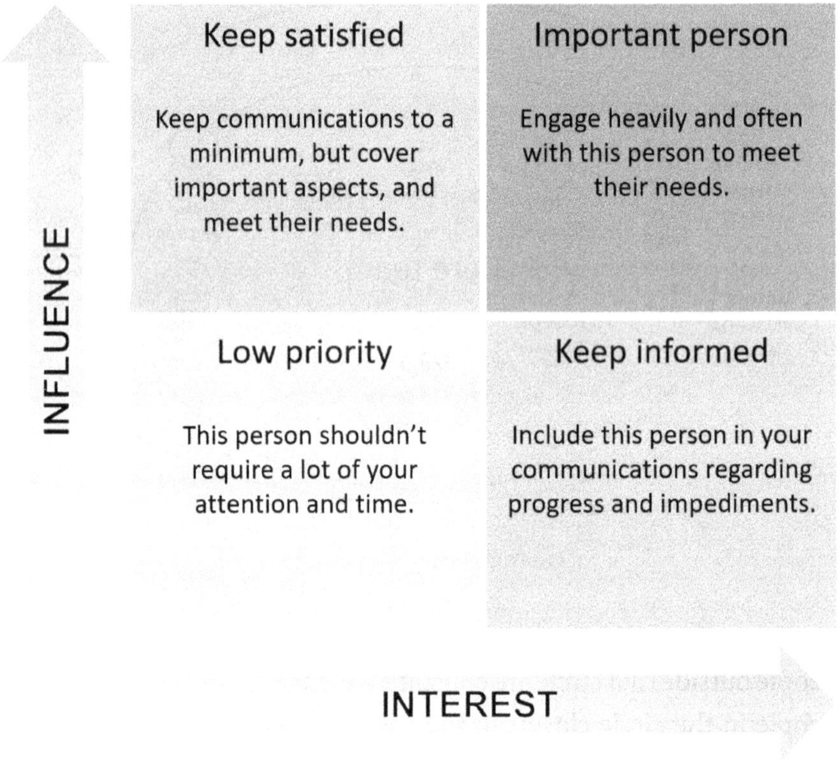

Keep satisfied	**Important person**
Keep communications to a minimum, but cover important aspects, and meet their needs.	Engage heavily and often with this person to meet their needs.
Low priority	**Keep informed**
This person shouldn't require a lot of your attention and time.	Include this person in your communications regarding progress and impediments.

INFLUENCE

INTEREST

Figure 7: Stakeholder influence map

You will need stakeholders' trust and confidence to succeed with your project, and the best way to do this is to be successful in delivery. The second-best way is to keep them aware of what is impacting delivery and your actions to prevent the project from failing.

I recommend meeting early with your more influential and interested stakeholders to understand their particular passion for the project. Find out how you can give them confidence and provide them with sufficient awareness of progress. This sets the foundation for communications that will maintain the support of these important stakeholders.

When you meet with them, set expectations about attending any Showcase your team conducts and other ceremonies. These are where you manage expectations and build their support. It is much better to have face-to-face conversations with your stakeholders than simply send them reports and emails.

Roles and responsibilities

Team cohesion is essential to good software delivery. You may not be directly responsible for this, but it can impact delivery and needs to be managed. Creating a RACI is a common approach for helping everyone understand their role and responsibilities. RACI is an acronym for Responsible, Accountable, Consulted, and Informed. It determines duties throughout the project. This clarification is essential, especially in large organisations with confusion or duplication between roles. It also helps confirm who holds different accountabilities and identifies escalation and delegation responsibilities.

When assigning new roles (such as Scrum Master), ensure that each person has a sufficient definition of their role and responsibilities and is trained to do it well. This can be a major issue when first moving to Scrum, as the new names and definitions are significantly different from traditional roles within software development teams. People can be easily confused or misguided if it is not clear. Mitigate this by doing an exercise with the team to allocate where responsibilities lie. It's especially useful in roles with similar responsibilities.

You will need to consider the roles (and associated responsibilities) your organisation has specified, as these cannot usually easily be relinquished or changed. Each person may have a bonus tied to their performance.

Figure 8: Deciding which roles have what responsibilities

Following the approach that a team should be self-organising, facilitate a session where individuals create sticky notes for what they believe should be their and others' responsibilities. Ask the group to discuss and agree on who will hold each responsibility. Take a look at figure 8 for an example. You can see that a flipchart sheet has been created for each role, and people add sticky notes representing the responsibilities each should have.

Social contracts help teams speed up the process of Forming, Storming, Norming, and Performing.

If you are forming a new team, or if some members are changing, it is essential to agree on how they will work together.

It is common in Agile for teams to form a *social contract*,[12] which explains how they behave, their values, and what happens if people stop meeting these expectations.

Creating a social contract helps teams speed up the well-accepted process of Forming, Storming, Norming, and Performing. It also helps newcomers understand how the team operates and what is important in maintaining cohesion when there are differing opinions or values.

Running Discovery workshops

Discovery is often run as one or more workshops where all relevant parties gather to discuss and decide what should be built and with what outcome in mind. The goal is to assemble everyone who can impact project decisions and go through the collated information to confirm understanding and agreement with the project scope and constraints.

Shared understanding means they are less likely to disagree later or change decisions that impact the delivery schedule. That's not to say that decisions *can't* be changed at any time, but it must be done with agreement and understanding of the impacts and trade-offs if meeting a deadline is essential. The Product Owner can often make scope decisions independently, but if the decision significantly impacts stakeholders, it might need their agreement.

You might consider splitting the Discovery process into a set of workshops and inviting people to attend those that are relevant to them. That way, you won't have essential stakeholders attending unnecessary sessions. For example, some won't be interested in how the technical solution is designed.

The team must understand the needs of your users and stakeholders before establishing their own. Your early Discovery workshops should capture the requirements of users and stakeholders, and later workshops gather the delivery team's technical requirements.

Throughout Discovery, your goal is to get agreement and alignment between various stakeholders about what needs to be built. Understand the constraints, the expected project outcomes, the ways of working, and who is expected to do what. If you run separate workshops with different stakeholders, circulate the outcomes as a summary. You may also need to walk individual stakeholders through particular artefacts if they are in their area of interest.

Empiricism: Scrum recommends that you adapt your software based on real world observation and learnings.

By the end of the Discovery process, you will want some representation of the known scope of work in a product backlog created by the delivery team.

That's not to say that the defined scope needs to be fully delivered — or that the backlog cannot grow as the team learns through empiricism and feedback. It's merely a starting point. Agile expects that the work is defined through inspection and adaptation of the software at regular intervals.

Preparation

You will need to be prepared for discussion and in-depth exploration in the Discovery workshops. The preparation doesn't need to be extensive, but, ideally, you will have the following:

- Provide any existing artefacts or documents that aid understanding and discussion of the upcoming work. These might include:

  ‣ Architecture and technical diagrams

  ‣ Business process diagrams

  ‣ Prototypes or early designs

  ‣ User interface designs

  ‣ Business rules or logic diagrams

- › Any existing software solutions that are relevant

- › Regulatory requirements, technical constraints or contractual obligations.

- Establish a space or environment where the attendees can concentrate on the discussion and not be distracted.

- Display artefacts on the walls and/or have copies available so people can easily discuss and write on them.

- Prepare other visual cues to elicit information from participants. These help people understand what is expected of them and limit the time required to capture the information.

- Hold interactive sessions to seek feedback and input. Ensure there is an easy way for people to share their input and for you (or a facilitator) to record it. A common way to share ideas and thoughts is to write on sticky notes and add them to artefacts or categories on the wall.

- If you collaborate online, find appropriate tools that can recreate the experience of sharing thoughts and ideas and artefacts as if they are in a room together. For example, use an online whiteboard tool.

- Invite everyone on a day where they don't have conflicts or distractions. Avoid intensive days when people are needed at their desks or on phone calls.

- Ensure that all relevant comments and information is recorded on the day. Arrange for a note taker and/or facilitator. If people document their thoughts with sticky notes, gather the results at the end of the workshop.

- Send out an agenda and supporting material, such as a project brief, so that people know why they are attending, the intended outcome of the workshop, and why their input is required.

- If any important stakeholders cannot attend, ask them to send a delegate who can make decisions on their behalf.

- Ensure that you invite the correct people to attend. You want to include:

  > The team(s) that will deliver the software solution

  > Any person who will fund the project and/or track costs closely

  > A representation of users and customers who can provide beneficial input that will determine the success of the software solution

  > Any additional stakeholders who define or decide project success, such as architects, practice managers, internal business staff, etc.

Process

When running your first Discovery workshop, it's helpful to have a facilitator act as a timekeeper, encourage people to contribute to the discussion and keep people focussed on the subject. This person usually opens the workshop by introducing themselves, walking through the agenda, and introducing each new speaker. The facilitator sets the expectations and works towards achieving the best outcome for the day. They do this by steering the conversation when required and directing people to complete activities.

An ice-breaker is a good way to start the first workshop, especially with a new audience.

These can be important as people in the workshop don't always know each other or feel safe speaking up. Introduce each person in some way to help everyone understand who they are, what their role is, and that their opinion is important.

An ice-breaker helps people feel like their views and opinions matter, and increases their likelihood of contributing.

An ice-breaker can be an interactive game that makes everyone contribute and (hopefully) have some fun. You can find plenty of examples on the internet.

The other benefit is that the ice-breaker encourages everyone to contribute. Often some people will avoid speaking or await the workshop's outcome. An ice-breaker can help them understand that everyone is expected to contribute.

Once the ice-breaker is completed, ask subject matter experts and stakeholders to explain particular aspects of the project. Often these experts will speak to some of the artefacts displayed on the walls. Topics may include; architecture, business domain and objectives, software design, legacy systems considerations, user interface design, customer needs, and user needs.

Limit the amount of time spent on each of these topics at the start, as they are designed to set context only. Typically, five to fifteen minutes is sufficient for each person to speak and answer questions. Sometimes this can be longer if you need to gain a wider context. One key stakeholder needs to explain the reason for embarking on this project. This is often done through a problem statement — a problem exists that requires a software team to build a solution to solve it.

The next major activity is asking people what it means for this software to be successful from their perspective.

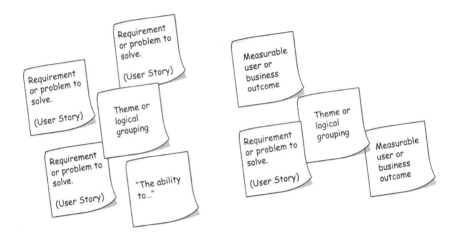

Figure 9: Free-form user and stakeholder requirements gathering

Give people time to define their requirements by posting them on a wall. The facilitator can go through these to clarify and confirm the requirement and note who wrote it. All this information will be collated as part of the set of requirements for the software solution.

It might be necessary to remove duplicates, and sometimes it's beneficial to group requirements into themes to be more manageable. Re-arrange them around these themes to show how they relate to each other. This adds valuable information and reduces the cognitive load on participants.

Consider setting up categories by business unit or department, as these can help interpret requirements and capture additional information. You can also categorise by persona if you know these for your software.

The diagram in figure 10 shows an example of letting users, stakeholders and customers define their early requirements. This will form the minimum set of high-level features they expect the software to offer. Not all of these requirements will make it into the solution, but it helps to have their initial expectations recorded somewhere so that they can be discussed.

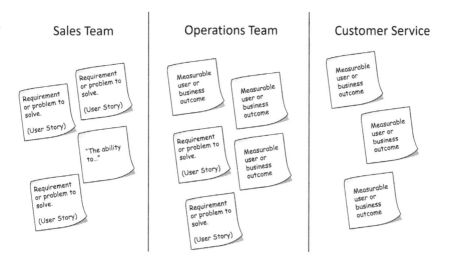

Figure 10: Categorise requirements by business unit or persona

Project Lisbon

Our stakeholders, users and customers can add features they want the software to provide.

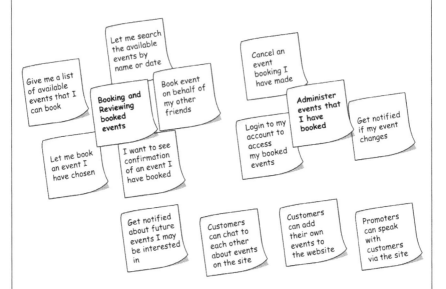

We now have a high-level set of features that should be considered part of the scope of work. Our list of features is:

- Give me a list of available events that I can book.

- Let me search the available events by name or date.

- Book event on behalf of my other friends.

- I want to see confirmation of an event I have booked.

- Let me book an event I have chosen.

- Cancel an event booking I have made.

- Login to my account to access my booked events.

- Get notified if my event changes.

- Get notified about future events I may be interested in.

- Customers can chat to each other about events.

- Customers can add their own events to the website.

- Promoters can speak with customers via the site.

This initial list may not sufficiently cover all the various aspects of the software solution, so it's useful to have other artefacts as prompts to explore the range of possible requirements. Your goal is to have a comprehensive, high-level list covering the full scope of work. It might look far more extensive and detailed than the worked example, which is okay. You should be able to identify high-level features and low-level requirements.

If there are user interface designs or wireframes, then it is often helpful to examine these in a meaningful manner and ask questions about each of the visible elements; What does this thing do? What happens when I do this? What happens if I haven't completed this, or I did it incorrectly? How do I learn what to do with this screen? Where is the data stored and retrieved from?

Ask the participants to place sticky notes on the designs, the business process diagram, or whatever artefacts are available. Doing so demonstrates that they have thought through how the software might work and triggers other participants to think of other things to add.

Project Lisbon

The facilitator can use artefacts like wireframes to ask as many probing questions as possible. They should encourage others to ask these questions, as each person has a different perspective that will identify even more requirements. The following image builds on the previous wireframe example and shows how it prompts people to add their requirements.

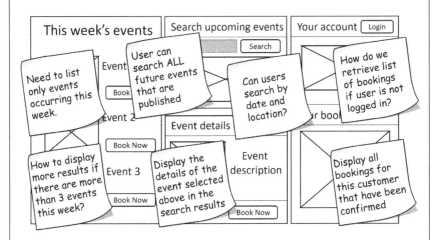

The participants should add any requirements they can imagine, problems they think will need to be solved, or questions they believe need to be answered. They can create sticky notes to add to the relevant screen element in the artefact.

This process will maximise the breadth of possible requirements and identify gaps in participant and team knowledge that need to be answered.

Aim to define all the high-level features rather than every little requirement in detail. Next, we will look at using the business process map artefact to record requirements.

Project Lisbon

Drawing a business process map allows the delivery team to add sticky notes representing elements needed for the software to work correctly. They should be thinking about the technical specifications of the software.

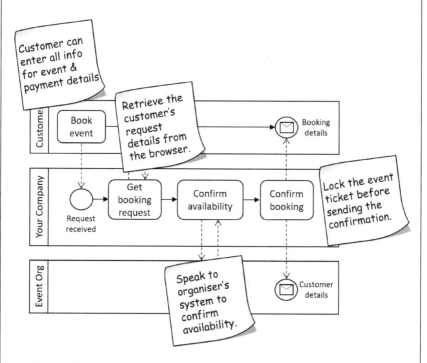

What we've gathered should be considered part of the scope of work. This might not be a finalised list, but it's a good starting point for designing the technical solution. Our list includes:

- Customers provide all the necessary information in some kind of form for the selected event and include their payment details.

- Retrieve the customer's booking details from the browser.

- Speak to the event organiser's booking system to confirm the availability of tickets for the customer's requested event.

- Lock a ticket allocation before sending the confirmation to the customer, so the ticket is guaranteed.

You should now have a high-level collection of work items. Two activities from here will help with backlog management. The first is to define the agreed scope of work. You might be able to rapidly de-scope requirements from the project, saving time and effort for you and the team. You can group features into three categories to help make scope decisions: In Scope, Out of Scope and Undecided.

The benefit of de-scoping items at this early stage is that it reduces the need to design solutions, break down work and provide estimates. Getting the participants to agree to de-scoping is a massive benefit for you and the team.

The second activity is to begin prioritising the backlog of work. The Product Owner is responsible for this. Ideally, a single person will be tasked with this, and they will be present in the Discovery workshop to conduct a first pass. You can choose to do this activity as part of a workshop with the other stakeholders present, and the Product Owner works with them to reach an agreement on priorities.

Alternatively, the Product Owner might be entrusted to manage the prioritisation process independently away from the workshop. If there are many requirements, this is probably best, as it will save time. Discuss and agree this with the Product Owner before the workshop.

Project Lisbon

Take this early opportunity to confirm (with your stakeholders) anything that is considered out of scope. Your team will save time by ignoring out of scope items from the solution design, planning and estimation.

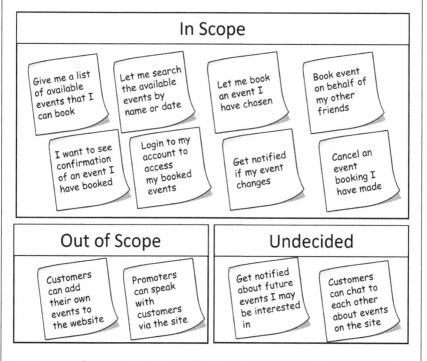

We now have a shortlist of eight features to deliver — and potentially two more if the undecided ones are brought into scope. Our reduced list of confirmed features includes:

- Give me a list of available events that I can book.

- Let me search the available events by name or date.

- Book event on behalf of my other friends.

- I want to see confirmation of an event I have booked.

- Let me book an event I have chosen.

- Cancel an event booking I have made.

- Login to my account to access my booked events.

- Get notified if my event changes.

The Product Owner

As we've noted, in Scrum, the Product Owner is responsible for prioritising the backlog. If you haven't already agreed on who that is, do so now before any further discussion about scope, prioritisation or schedule. This action avoids 'design by committee' — a well-known phenomenon where a group of people feels responsible for making important decisions but takes too much time, or they compromise and end up with a suboptimal solution.

> The **Product Owner** ensures that the project delivers value to the customer by regularly re-prioritising the backlog.

The Product Owner's responsibility is to set the vision for the product or software solution and then prioritise and adapt the product backlog to achieve the best outcome.

The Product Owner should represent the interests of the customer and the business stakeholders. Their role is to ensure that the project delivers value by prioritising high-value work first, then using Sprint Reviews to ensure that the working software has provided the anticipated value.

Dovetailing between projects

If your portfolio of work is made up mainly of independent projects, then your delivery team(s) will need to do Discovery ahead of each new project. Based on these findings, a project may be cancelled or delayed. For this reason, it is good to begin Discovery well ahead of delivery to gain confidence that the work will proceed.

If a project is cancelled or delayed, your team can minimise downtime by beginning Discovery on the next project in the queue.

Discovery of the next project should be started before the end of the current project to maintain momentum and to minimise downtime.

The ideal time to kick off the next project is immediately after the current one wraps up. That ensures that the delivery team does not sit idly waiting.

You want to guarantee that the next project will go ahead and that you have completed sufficient Discovery to know what work needs to be done. However, you don't want to disrupt the current project in case it drags out the timeline for completion.

The way to manage this careful balance is to dovetail the work. You do this by having one or two team members begin Discovery on the next project while the current project is reaching its conclusion. This might be disruptive, so plan for reduced capacity with your team during this period.

While they need not commit all their time to the task, one or two team members can pull together the artefacts previously described. If those artefacts do not exist, they can draft the documents and have early conversations with practice managers, architects and other stakeholders to understand the constraints for the next project and begin booking the workshops.

Throughout the Discovery process, the focus should primarily be on knowing if the project will go ahead, given the constraints, costs and desired outcomes. If a project is not viable, this is the time to stop, rather than once you've made a significant investment in building the solution.

The other focus during the Discovery process is to ensure that your team has adequate understanding of the software needs (at a high level) and the expectations of users and stakeholders, and the constraints they are working within.

You don't have to dovetail projects this way, but it is the best utilisation of your team.

Documentation

There is a balance between too much and too little documentation about the software, the solution, and the requirements. Agile states that it values *working software over comprehensive documentation*. The problem with comprehensive documentation is that it constantly needs to be updated, which adds no value to the customer and requires effort from your team. Only include those artefacts that help solve an existing problem, and only in sufficient detail to comprehend the problem and the solution and reach an agreement.

Most of the documentation your team writes will be User Stories that represent many discussions and decisions and are turned into working software. Software like Jira provides the ability to add comments to User Stories by various contributors. Your team can use this to capture the trade-off options and findings made along the way. That enables any newcomer to the project or team to review the conclusions and decisions and understand why they were made. It helps them quickly become productive and contribute without rehashing options and decisions.

The artefacts discussed in this book are designed to draw the bigger picture of what the software must provide to satisfy the customer's needs and the technical design. They assist the team to make decisions throughout the project.

CHAPTER FOUR

Breaking Down the Work

Traditional Waterfall projects end with a big bang and differ from the incremental Agile approach.

Breaking down the work enables us to implement the Agile principle that says delivery teams should be putting working software into the hands of the users as quickly as possible. *Deliver working software frequently, from a couple of weeks to a couple of months, with a preference for the shorter timescale.* This allows users to provide early feedback to the delivery team, who can then adapt the solution to meet their needs better.

The longer it takes to get the first increment of working software into users' hands, the greater the risk that what the team has built doesn't meet their needs and will require rework. And that ultimately impacts the delivery schedule and creates waste.

Your aim is to put working software into the hands of users as rapidly as possible.

Your goal then is to create a delivery schedule that delivers working software into the hands of users as rapidly as possible.

The software you release to users must be functional. That means it must deliver meaningful functionality, allowing them to accomplish their tasks and activities. It can't simply be an interface without a back end or missing vital elements that make it usable. As a guide, a user should be able to complete a meaningful user activity end to end. Examples might be generating a report, submitting a request or booking an event.

Vertical slicing

Software has historically been built in horizontal layers, like a cake, with each layer representing a different part of the technology stack. One layer might be the database, another the business or control logic and a third the user interface.

Individuals within a team might prefer to deliver the software in horizontal slices because it suits their expertise. For example, someone might be expert at creating databases and want only to do that. Modern engineers are expected to have skills across the full stack, allowing them to work in all aspects of the software. Building in horizontal layers requires completing large sections of the project before delivering working software to the users. If this is a problem in your team or organisation, speak with your management team about training engineers to have full stack skills.

A vertical slice of software provides end users with a meaningful piece of functionality.

We want to be able to create and serve our users a thin piece of the software, including all the horizontal layers required to deliver a functional slice. This gives the users enough of the software to be beneficial.

We call this a vertical slice, and it provides end users with a meaningful piece of functionality that they can use. The goal is to give your users and customers the earliest possible view of your working software and for them to offer valuable feedback that improves upon the work that has been completed.

An example of a vertical slice might be that the user can generate a report of how many customers have logged in. This piece of functionality might require that the user sets parameters that define the scope of the report, so it would include a form to submit their parameters for things like date range, customer type, etc.

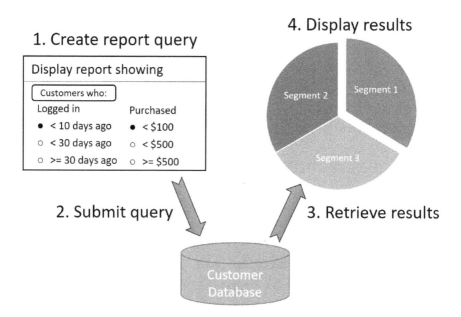

Figure 11: An example of an end-to-end vertical slice of software

The intended functionality might also allow them to change the format of the report between a web page, PDF, Excel, etc. A vertical slice means the user can generate the report from end to end. It might not satisfy all the expected options for the first increment (for example, it might initially only present the report in one format) until the user has indicated that the primary functionality is correct. Other formats can be added in later increments.

Another example might be that it may offer only the most commonly used criteria (instead of all possibilities) to generate the report, so the vertical slice is still usable in its first release.

Project Lisbon

A vertical slice should provide a working demonstration of one of the requested features. For example, *Let me search the available events by name or date.*

A vertical slice would allow the user to type in an Event name or an Event date. It would then retrieve all events that match the criteria and display them in a list.

This is a usable vertical slice of functionality.

This vertical slice might get refined over time to provide advanced behaviour for the user. For instance, the software might accept misspelled words or incomplete search words, or search results might start appearing while the user is entering a search term.

The first vertical slice should satisfy the original feature request at its most basic level. Further refinements and enhancements should be added once the user or customer confirms that the software performs the function as requested.

The product backlog

Receiving feedback and incorporating it into the software solution is one of the primary benefits of Agile delivery and a key contributor to meeting the definition of success. When creating your delivery plan, it is important to make allowances for receiving feedback which potentially becomes additional work items.

You can achieve this by creating a buffer in your estimated budget and schedule. For example, with the agreement of your sponsor, you might increase the estimated budget and timeline by twenty per cent. Another approach is to create a separate space in your product backlog for proposed enhancements. Any feedback from customers goes into this space, or bucket, for a future decision to make the enhancements. You might have an enhancement bucket for each Feature so that individual decisions can be made based on each Feature's popularity or value.

Product Backlog Items include any work items required to deliver working software. The product backlog is a single stack of ordered items, with the most valuable at the top and the least valuable at the bottom. Any new, unelaborated items created from feedback or learnings are also added to the bottom of the stack — at least until they can be prioritised. The least valuable items may never get completed, and that is okay.

The product backlog includes all work items required to deliver working software.

At the top of the stack, the items are the smallest and have greatest clarity, having been refined by the Product Owner speaking with users and customers. Things at the bottom of the stack have the least clarity and refinement and may need to be broken into smaller units.

The team aims to refine the most valuable work just in time before beginning to develop it. That means it occurs just before the Sprint in which the work will be completed.

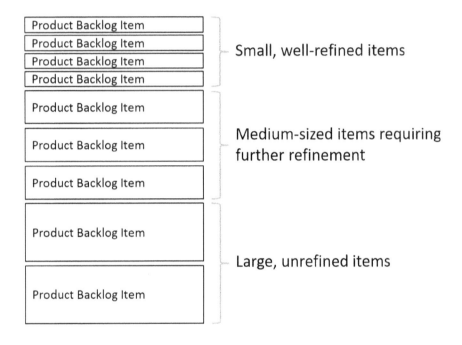

Figure 12: Example of a product backlog

Small items are at the top of the stack because they can be completed in a short timeframe. That means the team is more likely to deliver working software to users within a Sprint timebox.

At the bottom of the stack, the large items have not received any attention to understand, refine, or break down the work. Given they may never be completed, such efforts would be wasted.

Logical work structure

Even though the Product Backlog is described as a single stack of items, a logical hierarchy can be created representing the Work Breakdown Structure. In essence, it should represent the value to the user (or customer). That means that at each hierarchical level, the user can recognise the value of the individual work items at that level.

If you are working in a medium to large enterprise, your project will likely serve multiple purposes, including the needs of customers and the internal staff. Different components may be built to serve those individual purposes, and each one can be made independently. The order of building those components can be critical to the project's overall success.

Let's consider an example: a new software product is to be built for external customers. If the externally-facing product is built first and customers start using it immediately, it might create a massive overhead for back-office staff if the process of onboarding new customers requires manual effort.

Onboarding means creating and configuring accounts correctly, which involves communicating with the customer. The back-office staff might get overwhelmed, and customer experience may be impacted due to delays in onboarding. Therefore, the stakeholders for the project might choose to build software to automate the onboarding process first to reduce the overhead on back-office staff.

In this hypothetical example, the project has three major components: back-office onboarding automation, customer-facing product, and reporting functionality to help sales and marketing staff.

There are two ways to break the work down below project level.

The first is to represent the time-ordered components of the project. The second is to describe the functionality or value that benefits the user (or customer).

Time-based hierarchy

How you break down the project into time-ordered deliverables is for you, the Product Owner and your team to decide. Figure 13 demonstrates an example of such a hierarchy.

Some teams have Phase as the second level when delivering a large project that spans years. This allows a focus on delivering one component at a time and limits the conversation and the requirements to the current phase.

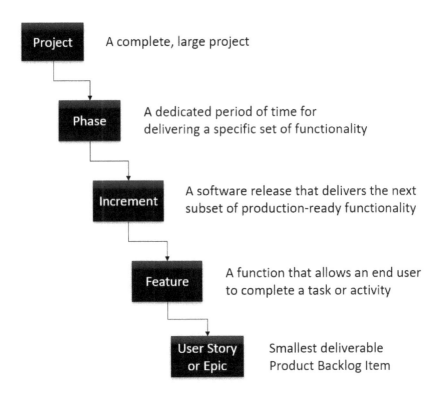

Figure 13: Creating a time-based hierarchy

A Phase can be considered an approximate timebox in which a particular group of functional items will be delivered. An example might be that your team decides to build the customer-facing functionality of a website, then automate back-office processes, and finally complete the reporting phase.

The typical next level should represent a software increment. For example, the first software release of user-facing functionality allows customers to begin using a new website. An increment at this level should allow a user to perform a complete end-to-end process.

From there, the next level might split an increment into particular Features that allow users to complete tasks. These could include logging in to a website, generating a graph on a report, or automating a business subprocess.

The final level should be User Stories or Epics. An Epic is simply a large User Story that needs breaking down further before being delivered.

Value-based hierarchy

With a value-based hierarchy (figure 14), you structure your backlog around the value delivered to the end user (or customer).

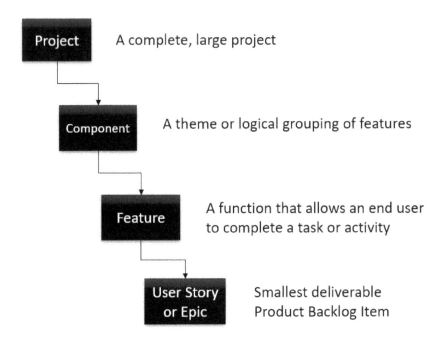

Figure 14: Creating a value-based hierarchy

The level below Project will likely be the Components of the software, which involve themes or groupings that serve different purposes. Much as a stereo system might include a music player, amplifier, and speakers, the components could group similar Features, such as Account Management, User Profile, Reporting, etc.

Next is a grouping of Features that the project delivers to the customer. You might be building a large number of software features and need to group them in a way that makes sense to the delivery team as well as to the end user.

Below the Feature level are Epics and User Stories — as described previously.

There are advantages and disadvantages to each method, and your team needs to decide which is best for them. Chapter Eight explains how Jira represents the logical hierarchy to help with delivery management and creating roadmaps.

Just-in-time refinement

User Stories are not the only way to capture the customer's requirements. Other methods include User Journey mapping, Empathy Mapping, Spec by Example, and Innovation Games. For brevity, I will focus on User Stories.

When your team is going through the early stage of Discovery and capturing requirements and problems to be solved, there's minimal detail in the User Stories. Remember, it's not only the Business Analyst or Product Owner's responsibility to capture User Stories. That belongs to the entire team, or at least representation from each team competency, for example, engineering, testing, analysis, and design.

A User Story is a placeholder for a later conversation that refines the User Story. The first time a User Story is created, it should have a simple statement describing the problem and why solving it matters. That will be sufficient for Product Owners to prioritise the item in the backlog, and for the team to get greater clarity of the requirement.

The common format for capturing a User Story on the first pass is:

As a *[persona]*, I want *[the ability]*, so that *[I can achieve this outcome]*.

The *persona* represents a particular type of user with a specific set of interests and tasks for which they use the software. A persona might be a booking manager, a reporting analyst, a customer service officer, etc.

The *ability* represents the functionality or feature they would like the software to have. For example, 'I want the ability to sort a large list of events by date'.

The *outcome* is why they want the functionality and helps the Product Owner understand the importance of the request. For example, 'So that I can see which events are occurring next week, and in what order they occur'.

Breaking down User Stories

The Backlog comprises Product Backlog Items, such as User Stories, Epics, Features, Spikes, etc. Making these items smaller requires breaking down the work. There is plenty of good content available on how to split User Stories, and I recommend studying that in detail if your team is struggling. Let's cover the basics, so you have a high-level understanding of the concepts before exploring them further.

INVEST

User Stories should deliver something that enables the user to perform a basic task, so they must offer some meaningful value, no matter how small. A simple acronym, INVEST, provides guidelines for creating a good User Story.

The term INVEST was coined by Bill Wake[13] as a reminder of the characteristics of a good quality User Story. It stands for:

Independent, Negotiable, Valuable, Estimable, Small, and Testable.

INVEST is a reminder of the characteristics of a good quality User Story.

Independent means each User Story can be completed on its own. The team is not required to complete other stories for one story to be considered complete.

Negotiable means the User Story can be changed. It is not written in stone and can be broken down into multiple other stories if needed.

Valuable means the User Story must deliver something beneficial to the end user or customer once completed.

Estimable means the User Story has enough detail and clarity that the team can provide some form of estimate. If they cannot do so, then the User Story requires further refinement.

Small means the User Story should be able to be completed in a short amount of time. You should aim for each story to be completed within a single Sprint. That way, the team won't carry stories from one Sprint to the next and is far more likely to release a working increment at the end of every Sprint. Ideally, the team can safely complete multiple stories during each Sprint.

Testable means the User Story is so clearly defined that tests can prove the story has been completed. It requires the story to be unambiguous, with a clear set of criteria that can be met and proven.

If the User Stories do not meet these INVEST criteria, the team needs to change how they have broken down the items.

Splitting a User Story

Use these questions to help your team break User Stories into smaller User Stories.

- Is the User Story a part of completing a business process? Can the team reduce the story to represent a single workflow step? Or can they follow just one small subprocess or path through the business process? Create separate User Stories for each alternative path or step.

- Does this User Story implement a set of validation logic or business rules? Can a single story represent a single rule or condition or a subset of rules?

- If this User Story requires a set of data variations to be tested, can the data sets be made smaller, either by data type or data subset?

- If this User Story covers a range of user interface options or variations, can it be reduced to represent one option or variation and then create stories for all others?

- If the User Story represents a complex solution, can a simpler version be created first and then add other stories to represent increasing complexity?

- If the User Story needs to meet difficult non-functional requirements such as speed or scalability, can a simplified version of the story be created first to satisfy the functional requirements, then generate other stories to meet the non-functional requirements?

- If the User Story needs to provide different results based upon the user type, date, location, etc., can a version of the story be created to satisfy one of those first and create separate stories for each of the other variations?

Finally, ask your team; 'How can this User Story be split and still satisfy INVEST?' With time they will become experienced and look for ways to do this themselves.

There is some great content online that explains how to break down user stories. Look for *The Humanizing Work Guide to Splitting User Stories.*[14] Gojko Adzic also has some excellent advice called *The Hamburger Method.*[15]

Story Points are a way of estimating the complexity, uncertainty, risk and the volume of work in a User Story.

Story Points measure the complexity, risk, uncertainty, and volume of work for a User Story and act as an estimate of effort for its completion. The measure is an abstract concept and doesn't convert into a measurable quantity in the real world. Instead, Story Points allow one piece of work to be compared to another to determine the difference in effort.

This can be a helpful tool for splitting User Stories because they indicate greater effort. Breaking down User Stories means you can isolate the parts of the story that require more effort.

When you separate low effort work from high effort work by splitting User Stories, the new set can be more easily prioritised by the Product Owner. They are looking to deliver high-value functionality with low effort, and then do higher effort items only once the customers/users confirm it is valuable enough.

A mature team can identify whether they can deliver a large proportion of the value with a fraction of the effort by splitting a User Story or Backlog Item in a particular way. We will explore Story Points and estimation in Chapter Five.

Delivering increments

Create a schedule of increments

You may experience challenges delivering the software in regular increments to your users and customers because they prefer to see a completed product or software project first. Use the following technique to work with these people and help them appreciate software delivered in increments.

While the logical representation of the product backlog is a single stack of User Stories, your customers and stakeholders will often want to know when they can start using the working software. They want to know which features will be available and in what order.

You can organise the development of the requirements in a logical manner that provides value to your users and customers while not having to perfect the functionality. Incremental releases allow you to improve it with each iteration. Note that typically a Product Owner would manage this activity, as they are responsible for selecting the value and the order that it is delivered in. Work closely with the Product Owner to create logical groupings and schedules for the working software.

Look at figure 15. Across the top is a list of Features that enable the customer or user to complete real-world activities. The group of items listed beneath each Feature represents the requirements or problems to solve to deliver that Feature, and the rows represent the incremental release of working functionality. Ideally, a user or business outcome will determine whether you have successfully met expectations with a release. These measurable outcomes contribute toward meeting the Product Goals.

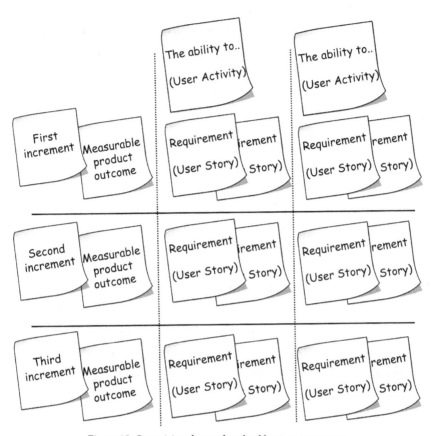

Figure 15: Organising the product backlog into increments

The desired interval for delivering working increments of software is at the end of every Sprint. While your team is still building their ability to break down work sufficiently, it might take multiple Sprints to deliver a working increment. In a mature Agile team, the team releases working increments at the end of every Sprint and receives feedback from customers each time. Work with your team to achieve this level of maturity — you might need to adjust the Sprint duration to better match the time required to deliver an increment.

Notice in the worked example below that the team continues to improve each Feature with each increment. The idea is to deliver a working Feature to be used by the user or customer, learn how to improve that Feature, and then do so iteratively. At some point, a Feature will not need further improvement, and the Product Owner can prioritise the next Feature to develop.

Project Lisbon

We can now add the Features and User Stories to the incremental release plan. We have added two core features to start with; *Let me search the available events by name or date*, and *Let me book an event I have chosen*. Under those Features are the User Stories needed to implement them. The first increment provides the most basic functionality to allow users to complete those two activities. The goal of the first increment is to enable the user to search and book an event. The second increment enhances the event search functionality to improve the user's ability to find an event.

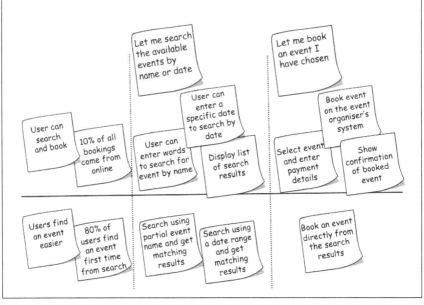

The first Increment should deliver one or more Features — sufficient to demonstrate how users complete their tasks and activities by using the software. Each successive Increment should continue to enhance the first set of Features and possibly add new ones. The Product Owner decides how to deliver value with each Increment.

Notice also that there is a separation between each Feature. If done correctly, they can be built and deployed in parallel by separate teams. Splitting the software project this way means it can be delivered more rapidly by additional teams.

Features can be built and delivered in parallel by separate teams to speed up delivery.

An excellent book explaining this process in detail is *User Story Mapping: Building Better Products Using Agile Software Design* by Jeff Patton.[16]

While the team is building the new product and seeking feedback from users and customers, the software may not provide sufficient functionality to be released for general use. The Product Owner should determine when it is ready to go live into production for anyone to use. You can also release it to a subset of users to seek broader feedback before it is available to general users.

CHAPTER FIVE

Estimation and Capacity

Traditional software projects usually include an expectation from the project sponsor to estimate how long the project will take to complete. Similarly, an estimate for a Feature or a requirement is often about time.

Scrum is best suited to product development, where the focus is on satisfying the customer rather than on time-based estimates. Agile's approach is that you continue to iteratively build the product or feature while value can be added. That creates a conundrum for people in delivery roles who are expected to provide time-based estimates for their projects.

Stakeholders need to understand that if the scope of work changes throughout the delivery of the project, then time-based estimates cannot be accurate or reliable.

If the **scope of work** changes throughout the delivery of the project, then time-based estimates cannot be accurate or reliable.

An easy approach to accounting for variability is to double or triple any estimate your team creates and give that to your stakeholders. I don't recommend this because over-estimation is often perceived as bad as under-estimation, plus your stakeholders are looking for reliable information.

There are different ways of estimating timelines while still using an Agile approach, and we will explore some of them in this chapter. There is plenty of good content available online for specific estimation techniques, so I won't cover these in detail. Planning Poker[17] is one of the more popular methods.

Principles of estimation

Let's start by understanding some foundational principles of estimation.

The first principle is that no software development estimate is entirely accurate because there are too many unknowns and variables. That said, some estimates are more accurate than others and typically took more effort to investigate the work.

The path to providing an extremely accurate estimate upfront usually includes the following steps:

- Capture all of the requirements — upfront and in detail.
- Break down the size of the work items small enough that the effort to complete each one is obvious. Think small as in hours, not days, weeks or months.
- Ask the team to estimate every individual item.
- Resolve all of the unknowns about the work items through investigation and experimentation.

- During delivery, limit the impact of risks, issues, dependencies, impediments, etc., so that they can be resolved or accepted immediately.

- Remove the ability to change the scope entirely.

- Ensure complete consistency of the make-up of the team and the type of work throughout the project.

- Prevent anything that disrupts the team.

- Ensure the team has maturity with the technology they are working with.

When you look at that list, you can imagine a Waterfall delivery model where everything is expected to be known and understood in advance. The team works on a fixed scope of work and has no flexibility around what is built.

The conclusion here is that asking for accurate estimates makes the team work in a Waterfall model, and prevents them from taking an Agile approach to delivery. This is worth communicating to your stakeholders. If Agile delivery is important, then stakeholders must forgo some certainty in terms of time and cost.

Accurate estimates are counterproductive for the following reasons:

- The team must spend significant time doing activities that do not deliver customer value.

- Estimates for the entire project are invalid if the scope of work can change (as it does in an Agile environment).

- Estimates will rarely match the reality due to the variables, inconsistency and uncertainty inherent in any software project.

- Providing a more accurate estimate usually doesn't change anything.

- An accurate estimate is usually designed as a constraint that limits innovation and experimentation, which is counterproductive in Agile delivery.

The second principle is that the team delivering the software needs to estimate the work. Sometimes a project manager or a PMO (Project Management Office) estimates the work based on their understanding. That is not effective — either as an estimate or as a target.

No estimate is completely accurate when it comes to software development.

The PMO can sometimes be responsible for forming project teams and assigning enough people to meet the estimates. In Agile, your organisation should have long-standing teams that don't often change. This improves team collaboration, builds domain knowledge and improves delivery and estimation.

The Delivery team will have the best understanding of what work is required to deliver the software, assuming they have been through a Discovery process. They also have the best ability to estimate the work — assuming that they have previous experience with the technology, existing systems and ways of working. The secondary benefit of having the Delivery team estimate the work is that they will take greater accountability for meeting the estimate.

Estimates do provide some value to stakeholders and sponsors. They need a sense of the project's viability in terms of the cost and effort compared against the value that it will deliver. If the perceived value does not exceed the cost and effort sufficiently, the project should be cancelled or delayed until circumstances change. This is good governance and avoids forcing teams into delivering impossible projects with unrealistic time and cost constraints.

The delivery team can provide a high-level estimate for the work to guide your sponsors and stakeholders in making their decision. In the next section, I will discuss an Order of Magnitude which gives that high-level estimate.

The third principle is that the first estimate given to a stakeholder or sponsor tends to be the one they hold you accountable to, especially if it's favourable to them. If it isn't, they will likely challenge the estimate and ask how you and the team came up with it.

For this reason, be extremely mindful about any first estimate, especially with the language you use. If you say 'It should take about six months', that will get thrown back to you with far greater certainty than you intended. Sponsors and stakeholders are accountable for ensuring that your project is cost-effective and the best use of the team's time. They will prefer a low estimate because it offers a good outcome for them. Once you have provided an estimate, they often see that as a commitment from you (and perhaps the team) and will aim to constrain your project to those parameters.

Your better option is to be vague with any first estimate (unless you have spent the time building confidence) and speak in terms of a range. For example, you might say, 'It could take anywhere between six and twelve months'. Then when they try to claim 'You said it would take six months', you can respond with 'Or anywhere up to twelve'. When they say that this is too vague, or not accurate or certain enough, explain that you need to conduct Discovery workshops to arrive at a more narrowed range.

Order of magnitude

An Order of Magnitude (OOM) is designed to give a broad approximation as a high-level estimate. It uses language intentionally designed to avoid certainty or accuracy. Your first and initial estimate is often used to assess whether a project (or a Feature) is worth pursuing. If it is too high, then, hopefully, that will be sufficient for your stakeholders or sponsors to decide not to continue. Alternatively, it might lead to further questions about bringing the estimate down. At that point, you can talk about conducting further Discovery to limit the scope and technical solutions and better meet a desirable estimate.

The simplest and least-informative type of OOM is T-shirt sizing. With this approach, you ask your team how would they describe the project. Is it Extra Small, Small, Medium, Large or Extra Large?

This information might not be enough to decide whether to proceed with the project. If so, ask for T-shirt sizing of historical projects that the team have been a part of. Now you have relative sizing where the current estimate is related to something already completed. If the team is reluctant to choose a T-shirt sizing category, you can simply ask, 'Would you say that this project is bigger than this previous project or smaller?' and then ask, 'How much bigger/smaller?'

The next level of detail when providing an OOM is to give a range, and, hopefully, your team has enough information and experience to do so. You might propose options: 1 to 3 months, 3 to 6 months, 6 to 12 months, 12 to 24 months, or greater than 24 months. Notice that the ranges increase in size as the timeframe increases? That is because longer and larger projects have greater uncertainty due to the increased likelihood of things changing in that timeframe and because of the number of unknowns.

The next level of detail when providing an OOM is to give a different kind of range. This gives an approximate number of weeks or months, and then applies a range of variability — usually in the form of a per cent. For example, this project is estimated to take six months, plus or minus fifty per cent, meaning the project could be completed three months earlier, or three months later, than the six-month estimate.

I do not recommend providing narrowed accuracy for inexperienced teams, as this might give stakeholders a false sense of certainty. Wait until the team has delivered at least one project before offering greater accuracy.

If your team has completed sufficient Discovery, and is still not confident with their estimate, then do some activities to identify and unpack the cause of their uncertainty. Use methods to remediate or manage them, and try estimating again. We'll cover this in Chapter Six: Planning to Avoid Failure.

When providing any form of estimate, include any assumptions, constraints, and dependencies used. This protects the team in case those things change or don't occur as expected, and it is part of managing your stakeholders.

When giving an estimate, include any assumptions, constraints, and dependencies that were used by the team.

If your stakeholders are still demanding revision of the estimate for accuracy, the best way forward is to break the work into smaller components and provide an OOM for each one.

Next level of estimation

Stakeholders and sponsors may seek to use estimates to constrain costs and schedules, which goes against Agile values and principles and should be avoided. You can discuss with your stakeholders and sponsors the importance of having an adaptive budget and timeframe that allows for building software that delivers on project outcomes *and* the customer's needs.

You can propose alternatives to meeting all scope within a deadline. For instance, the team stops delivering increments when time and budget run out. Alternatively, deliver the scope in the backlog, starting from the most valuable to the least valuable backlog item, until time or budget runs out. Your team will deliver working software, but it may not include all the expected features and functionality.

That may not satisfy your stakeholders because it doesn't tell them how many features or increments will be completed within a given timeframe or budget. At this point, you can propose that the team will provide an OOM for individual features, then combine those to estimate how many might be completed within a given timeframe or budget.

An **elaborated story** that is ready for the next Sprint is when the team can provide the most accurate estimate.

Doing this helps your stakeholders become more comfortable with Agile delivery. As your organisation becomes more familiar and comfortable with Agile delivery, you can start taking steps to reduce the need to estimate whole projects. You can begin to provide a roadmap of planned Features with approximate time ranges for delivery.

Before starting the next Feature in the queue, ask the team to break the Feature into User Stories. They could supply initial Story Point estimates before starting the Feature or provide estimates only once the story has been elaborated and is ready to be planned into a Sprint. That is when the team can provide the most accurate estimate.

As the team becomes more familiar with the work and each other, their accuracy at the story level will improve. Their estimates will be the most accurate by the end of the project, assuming they focus on improving accuracy.

Using Story Points to estimate

Story Point estimates require two conditions to be valid and useful. The first is a reliable history of the team's Story Point estimates. This is missing in a new team, so it's hard if you start a project with a group that hasn't worked together. I recommend that you follow the Scrum process, asking the team how much work they believe they can safely complete in a Sprint and commit to that as a starting point. With each consecutive Sprint, refine their commitment based upon the previous Sprint. Story Point estimates must be at team level and for a specific team to be useful.

Story Points are commonly used to estimate a team's capacity in Scrum; however, they are not discussed in the Scrum guide. Regardless, they help teams plan their Sprint workload. The idea of Story Points is that they give a numeric value to the perceived effort of completing User Stories.

That number is usually provided in relation to historical experience – you try to relate one User Story to another where you know the approximate effort required to complete the historical story. The idea is that you can measure the number of Story Points your team finished in the previous Sprint, then allocate a similar amount of effort for the next Sprint.

The Story Points completed per Sprint are known as Velocity, and this should be reasonably consistent from Sprint to Sprint. It is rare that everything remains so, which affects the certainty and reliability of Story Point estimates.

Velocity can be impacted by team changes, absence of team members, impediments, changes in the type or domain of work, increasing complexity, and team cohesion and engagement. Hopefully, you can see that providing estimates based on the most recent historical evidence is no guarantee that the future capacity or throughput of the team will remain the same.

You may find that people attempt to convert Story Points into time-based estimates, usually to get an estimate in hours or days for a requirement or User Story. Again, this is the wrong approach and will get inconsistent results for the reasons explained earlier. The purpose of Story Points is to measure the perceived effort of completing a User Story, incorporating complexity, risk, uncertainty and the volume of work. Effort does not translate linearly into time. All these factors will impact the time required to complete the story differently.

Epic-level estimation

My preferred approach to estimating a project (if you are required to track progress against an upfront estimate) is to ask the team to provide preliminary estimates at the Epic level.

After building a backlog of work, you should have a set of features that need to be built. These can be broken into a collection of high-level Epics, each of which must be independent and clear enough to the team that it can be given a preliminary estimate.

We say *preliminary* because it is an estimate without sufficient details for a meaningful assessment.

If the Epic contains a lot of uncertainty, complexity, or risk, the team should assign higher Story Points to represent this. Ideally, not all Epics have very high Story Points. You may need to challenge the team to think a little harder if they do.

While the estimates for each Epic will be reasonably inaccurate at this stage, hopefully, the inaccuracies — both higher and lower — will balance each other out. You should end up with a reasonable approximation of the effort required to deliver the whole project. There will always be variability that you will want to allow for by using a range, for example, plus or minus thirty per cent. This initial Epic level estimate will give you a base figure to track progress against.

Using throughput to estimate

An alternative to estimating effort in Story Points is to use Throughput, which counts the number of work items completed within a Sprint. The benefit is that it takes the subjectivity, or opinion, out of estimation. Story Points represent the opinion of the delivery team, whereas Throughput represents the objective count of completed items.

The **benefit of using Throughput** is that it takes the subjectivity out of estimation.

Although Throughput is an objective measure, it still has a lot of potential variability due to the nature of the work items. Some items are larger or more complex and generally require more time to complete. That means the number of completed work items may vary dramatically between Sprints.

You can improve estimation by Throughput by breaking down work until all items are similarly sized. The advantage here is that it reduces the variability of time to complete work items. This process can take a lot of training and support and will be covered in my next book.

To estimate a project or Feature, break down all work items into User Stories in the backlog, and then measure the average number the team can complete in a specific time frame, usually a Sprint. If the team is reasonably consistent, you need only divide the number of items in the backlog by the number of items they can complete in a Sprint to get the number of Sprints required to complete the work. Again, this doesn't account for the variability of scope or the size of the items in the backlog. If the User Stories (or Epics) in the backlog need to be broken down into smaller User Stories, this increases the number of items in the backlog.

Capacity planning

Capacity planning simply determines how much work is expected to be completed within a timeframe. Some Agile teams use average historical Velocity to determine the anticipated capacity of the following Sprint. Take the average Velocity of the three most recent Sprints to remove some of the variability, and you will have a reasonable estimation of the capacity of the next one.

That assumes that people's availability doesn't change — if team members take leave or meetings impact their work, this will change the capacity of the Sprint. It's important to use Velocity from recent Sprints, not the distant past, as too many things can change over longer periods.

Delivery teams can use capacity planning when planning large pieces of work that span across multiple Sprints. If a team is doing a quarterly plan, they would typically plan out six Sprints (based on two-week Sprints) and allocate their typical Velocity to each Sprint. We will cover this in more detail in the section on Quarterly planning.

By measuring capacity based on historical measurement, you can begin to predict and plan future capacity beyond the next Sprint. The further ahead, the more inaccurate the prediction due to the increasing likelihood of change.

> Use **capacity planning** when planning large increments of work that span across multiple Sprints.

This can provide an alternative to upfront estimation.

Alternative to upfront estimation

As your stakeholders become reasonably familiar with Agile and iterative delivery, they may be comfortable with receiving regularly updated forecasts that represent the anticipated completion date for the known scope. This will give a more accurate representation because it is based on the most up to date information. The accuracy of the team's Story Point estimates also improves over time.

Velocity-based forecasting

An alternative to an upfront estimate is to provide a forecasted completion date based upon the current known scope of work and the recent Velocity of the team. I call this *forecast modelling*.

You might already be familiar with the burn-down chart in Agile that shows the number of Story Points completed and the number awaiting completion. It is usually within the constraint of a Sprint timebox. It works because the number of Story Points is known at the start of the Sprint, assuming the team has estimated the Sprint backlog items in Story Points.

The burn-up chart is similar to the burn-down chart. It shows the number of completed Story Points for a Project, Feature, or Increment. The number is cumulative — it continues to increase as the project progresses and User Stories are completed. The burn-up chart doesn't have a timebox; instead, the chart accrues over time.

The burn-up chart has a second line that tracks the estimated scope. It helps stakeholders see how scope changes over time and how the team is tracking towards completion of the estimated scope items.

The graph in figure 16 shows two lines representing completed work items and the total scope of work. The measurement of work effort is in Story Points, and the timeline is measured in Sprints. The dotted line at the end of the line representing Completed work items is the forecast projection of Velocity. The forecast completion date of the work is where the two lines intersect. We can predict that if the Total Scope and average Velocity remain the same, the team should have completed the work by the end of Sprint 15.

The burn-up chart is updated at the end of every Sprint to show the increased amount of completed work, how the Total Scope has changed, and how the projected Velocity has changed.

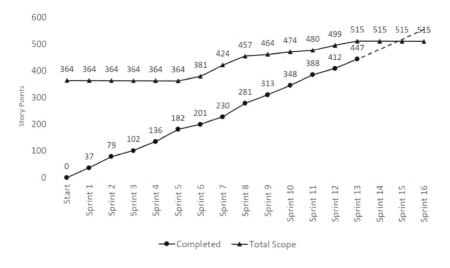

Figure 16: Velocity-based forecast example

Probabilistic forecasting

Another alternative to providing an upfront estimate is to create a probabilistic forecast of when the work will be completed. This requires knowing the number of work items in advance, as well as the typical throughput of the delivery team. This will be based on a timebox such as one week or one Sprint. Again, use recent historical data to determine the typical throughput.

A probabilistic forecast provides a set of probability outcomes against a range of dates. It allows you to choose what level of certainty you and your stakeholders are willing to accept.

A **probabilistic forecast** provides a set of probability outcomes against a range of dates.

121

Monte Carlo is an accepted model for generating this forecast, using sampling of historical data to arrive at a result that covers the full range of likelihoods. Bear in mind that the algorithm is only as good as its data. Since it is based on throughput, it has the same limitations as previously identified.

The following table shows an example that suggests the imagined project will be completed within twenty-three weeks.

Likelihood (0 - 100%)	Duration (weeks)	Date of completion	
100%	23	2/12/2023	High certainty of completion within 23 weeks of starting.
95%	20	11/11/2023	
90%	19	4/11/2023	High likelihood of completion within 19 weeks of starting.
85%	18	28/10/2023	
80%	17	21/10/2023	
75%	17	21/10/2023	
70%	16	14/10/2023	
65%	16	14/10/2023	
60%	16	14/10/2023	
55%	15	7/10/2023	
50%	15	7/10/2023	
45%	15	7/10/2023	
40%	15	7/10/2023	
35%	14	30/09/2023	
30%	14	30/09/2023	
25%	13	23/09/2023	
20%	13	23/09/2023	
15%	13	23/09/2023	
10%	12	16/09/2023	
5%	11	9/09/2023	No chance of completion within 9 weeks of starting.
0%	9	26/08/2023	

Figure 17: Monte Carlo example of probability-based forecasting

This method works best when all work items are small and approximately the same size. Greater variability of size results in more uncertainty.

Improving estimation

The Cone of Uncertainty

'At the beginning of a project, comparatively little is known about the product or work results, so estimates are subject to large uncertainty. As more research and development is done, more information is learned about the project, and the uncertainty then tends to decrease.'[18]

The Cone of Uncertainty model says we increase the certainty of our estimates over time as the project progresses. That is the result of our research, learnings from observation of the project progress, continuous improvements, and from breaking down and elaborating the work.

I have adapted the original Cone of Uncertainty (figure 18) to visualise the work breakdown and how it aligns to increasing certainty. The process as described is:

- We begin by receiving a new Project Brief — a high-level summary of intent. We have very little information at this stage, so no ability to estimate the effort to deliver the project.

- Next, we perform Discovery, and from that process, we understand the desirable functionality that may (or may not) be included in the final software product. At this point, we can provide an Order of Magnitude for the whole project or individual Features. We have improved our ability to estimate the project, but it's still not completely accurate.

- Now we can break down the Features into Epics or directly into User Stories. Without fully elaborated User Stories, we are still not able to provide accurate estimates. However, the team should be able to provide preliminary estimates in Story Points if it helps prioritise the backlog.

- Finally, the stories are elaborated (defined at a detailed level, including criteria for their successful completion). Each story can be broken into tasks that the delivery team needs to undertake to complete the story. Here we have the greatest level of certainty and estimation accuracy. The value of estimating in Story Points at this stage is to indicate what stories the delivery team believes they can complete in a Sprint. They are not intended to be converted into time-based estimates.

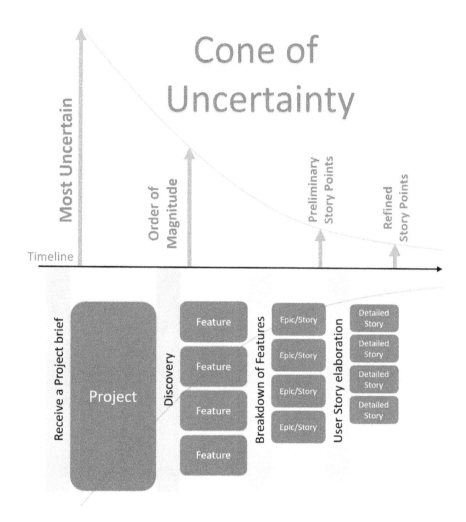

Figure 18: Cone of Uncertainty

If you are considering applying the Monte Carlo method, I recommend that you split the initiative into either Epics or User Stories and use that data to run your simulation. Remember, smaller is better with Monte Carlo, so User Stories will give a superior result. You don't need to have elaborated them but you need a fairly complete list covering the breadth of the entire project. You can also run the Monte Carlo simulation over an individual Feature rather than the entire project. This should achieve a more accurate result because there is greater clarity of requirements in just one Feature, and the duration is shorter for delivering a Feature than an entire project.

CHAPTER SIX

Planning to Avoid Failure

Risk mitigation and problem resolution should be a daily activity for a Scrum team. The Daily Scrum, Sprint Planning, and the Sprint Review are all there to identify risks and determine how they can be managed.

When creating a longer-term plan for your team and the project, you have an opportunity at the outset to identify problems that could impact outcomes. Before beginning delivery, take this opportunity to identify risks and reduce their impact by incorporating them into your plan.

Identifying and reducing risks

A Post-Implementation Review is a good activity for Project Managers and PMOs to conduct after completing a project. It allows the team, the managers and the stakeholders to examine how well the project went, how it achieved expected outcomes, and what improvements might be needed for future projects. This is like a Retrospective, but it applies to the whole project — and only once it is completed.

> A **Pre-mortem** tries to determine the cause of failure before a project begins as a way to prevent failure.

Sometimes these are known as Post-mortems when a project has gone badly, and people need to understand the causes to prevent similar outcomes in the future. If a recent Post-mortem or Post-Implementation Review involved your team, that is a good starting point for determining issues that need to be resolved for the next project.

An activity to run before kicking off the project is a *Pre-mortem*. The idea behind this is that we ask the delivery team and stakeholders (and possibly the users), 'If we roll forward to the end of this project and imagine that the project has failed, can you tell me what was the cause of it going wrong?' You then ask each person to contribute their opinions — which will likely be based on real historical events. This is useful if you are unfamiliar with delivering projects with this team or group of stakeholders.

The phrase *Pre-mortem* might be too dramatic and cast a negative vibe over the project, so you may choose different terminology. But the principle is valid — if the project was to fail, what are the likely causes?

Identifying problems

You need to have completed Discovery, Solutioning and Estimation to get a good result from this exercise. The team will need this information to decide how the outcome will likely turn out. If they are under pressure from technical complexity or unrealistic timelines, they will only be able to provide information for the next activity once they have completed the earlier steps in this book.

It is good practice to use categories as a prompt to ask people for their thoughts and opinions. Problems that occur in delivery tend to fall into one of the following categories:

- Risks: something known that may cause problems

- Issues: something known that will cause problems

- Dependencies: a constraint that is out of the control of the team

- Assumptions: something assumed that might change and cause a bad outcome

- Unknowns: something that the team is aware of but doesn't understand that may cause a bad outcome.

Place these categories where the team can contribute their thoughts and opinions, and ask them to include their name on each item they add. Read each one to confirm the categorisation, and ask the contributor to clarify the item for the group, as needed.

Managing problems

Once the team has listed and confirmed the items, incorporate them into the delivery plan. This will help remediate them and increase the certainty of achieving a successful outcome.

Risks represent events that might occur and would impact the delivery of the planned outcome. When preparing a delivery plan or an estimate, raise anticipated risks that can impact the project outcome, and then add activities into the plan that reduce the likelihood or impact of the risk.

The first option is to *resolve* the risk ahead of time. When you ask for ideas to do so, someone will likely think of a solution that requires some activity or work. If the team can resolve it themselves, add an item to the product backlog that resolves the risk. If the team cannot do so, it might need to be escalated to other parties who can.

The second path is to *mitigate* the risk, which means to put in place a plan or activity that aims to minimise the severity of the risk — if and when it occurs. An example might be that a person on your delivery team has specific knowledge, and if they are absent, the team is blocked. A way to mitigate this risk is to share the person's knowledge by documenting it or passing it on to others. This might also result in creating a backlog item to do the work.

The third way is to *accept* the risk, not address it. By listing it as an acceptable risk, you will have managed stakeholder expectations that you and the team are aware of the risk and accept the impact if it does occur.

Issues are similar to risks, but they differ in that they generally have occurred or are expected to occur at some future point. You treat them like a risk, except that they are expected to happen.

Dependencies must be incorporated into the delivery plan because they are highly likely to cause a bad outcome unless monitored and managed.

As with risks, you can manage dependencies by resolving, mitigating or simply accepting them. For the first two options, include something in the backlog representing the work needed to address the dependency. It's also valuable for you (in your delivery role) to track these dependencies, as they tend to be time-bound, and you'll need to manage them at specific times.

Assumptions should be easy to address because they represent something the team or stakeholders know and are either true or not.

You can test the truth by conducting an activity. Sometimes you can do this whenever you choose, but sometimes you must wait because particular things need to occur first.

Add a work item to the backlog for the team to confirm the assumption. If it is technical, the team can add a Spike, which is an activity that the team conducts to explore such solutions. That will confirm that the assumption is true or false, at which point the learnings can be accommodated into the delivery plan.

Unknowns are hard to deal with because they cannot be immediately confirmed, and their impact is unknown.

Unknowns are things that people can raise, which may or may not be a problem. They should be thought through to find any implications for the project. You might choose to make an assumption about the unknown and then incorporate it into the backlog as needing confirmation.

For example, the team doesn't know if they need to test their code for security in a project. You can turn this into an assumption by stating that the team must do so and confirm later whether that is true or false.

Add these problems to the backlog as work items for the team to address, incorporating their management into your delivery plan.

One benefit of conducting this activity with the team is that they begin to consider these when planning or solutioning. Over time, the team becomes more autonomous and self-managing by raising and addressing issues without being prompted.

Confidence vote

Once your team has incorporated the known constraints and complexities into the plan, ask how confident they feel about completing the project.

A confidence vote could be as simple as thumbs up or down, or more elaborate, with each person giving a rating out of five. The specific result is not important — what matters is that the team is confident they have a workable plan that allows them to achieve the expected results.

The exercise also reveals who is still uncertain so that you can find out why. There might still be concerns that have not been dealt with or items not raised because they are beyond team or individual control. You now have an opportunity to capture those items and consider how to address them.

Consider running a confidence vote before and after the exercise to identify and address risks and issues. Hopefully, the team becomes more assured that the plan is achievable.

Escalation and risk management

Escalation

The team will raise risks and issues they cannot manage, which must be escalated to management and stakeholders.

In large organisations, projects will usually have a steering committee that meets regularly to receive progress updates and reports of risks and issues that impact the project. You would typically present escalated items to them as they can decide to resolve things that the delivery team cannot.

For example, one matter that the team cannot manage is having sufficient people to complete the work in the expected timeframe. The steering committee should have the authority to engage additional people. If your organisation does not have steering committees to oversee projects, then your next option is the management team, which should be able to address escalated items.

Stakeholders might also need to be aware of these items, as they have an inherent interest in the project's outcome and any impact that may affect it.

Risk management

A mature organisation that runs multiple projects will usually hold a risk management forum on a semi-regular basis. This forum is for escalating, tracking and managing risks and issues that the delivery team cannot resolve and usually includes people with authority to make decisions and action change.

If your organisation doesn't have a risk management forum, speak with the management group or the PMO to set one up. It is a good way of managing stakeholders and the management team's expectations for project delivery.

However, the forum should be a last resort for addressing items that arise, as the infrequency of meetings and delays in resolving escalated items can mean a team is blocked for weeks.

Influence and support

The information above on risk identification and management is good practice. But in some organisations, it is not always that straightforward. Large organisations can run multiple projects

Your project can be put at risk by other projects that are running simultaneously.

at once. Those projects can impact each other when numerous projects depend upon the same set of resources, whether that represents computing environments, key people, business stakeholders, or software licences.

Other projects can put your project at risk too, which means that standard procedures for addressing problems may not work.

If you have exhausted typical avenues for escalating and resolving items, look more broadly at your set of stakeholders. Someone in your organisation should care about your project's success and help by supporting you to fix things.

That person needs to have a strong *interest* in the successful outcome and substantial *influence* to change things. Revisit your stakeholder map to see who meets these criteria, and if nobody does, use your network to find the right person.

Explain your situation and the likely impact of being unable to resolve an item. Make it clear that you have exhausted your alternatives, and they are your last option. If a successful outcome is critical to them, they will make whatever change is necessary to resolve your item.

It is essential and valuable to understand who is ultimately accountable for particular outcomes. In your stakeholder map and RACI, you have identified who has accountability for the successful delivery of the project. You might have the *responsibility*, but someone else likely has the *accountability*. That person has the best interest in resolving escalated issues.

CHAPTER SEVEN

Longer-term Planning

A longer-term vision and plan for project delivery help identify and actively pre-empt upcoming issues and impediments. The plan also enables you to track the progress of deliverables against timelines (and possibly deadlines) and make changes where needed.

Scrum doesn't provide this level of planning, which is where most of the challenge exists for teams learning the framework. For further explanation about the exclusion of longer-term planning, you can read *Gone Are Release Planning and the Release Turndown* at https://www.scrum.org/resources/gone-are-release-planning-and-release-turndown.

Rolling Wave planning

Rolling Wave Planning is the process of gradually increasing the level of detail in the plan as more information becomes available. Rather than defining and detailing a complete project plan

Rolling Wave plans provide greater detail about the immediate future and less later.

upfront, the rolling wave provides greater detail about the immediate future and less later.

Ninety-day planning

It is common to use a ninety-day rolling wave, which represents approximately three months. You and your team should know, in reasonable detail, which major aspects must be considered in that period: releases, integration testing, environment changes, people changes, dependency realisation, etc. Anything in the schedule beyond ninety days can be left until later as it is likely to change.

Wave planning provides higher-level and longer-term vision for the team.

The plan manages typical project resources, including additional people or support from experts, environments, and dependencies. You want a high-level view of the plan for this period, with enough detail to know where and when to ask for more specifics.

That doesn't replace Sprint planning, which is at a very low level of detail and core to the success of Scrum. Wave planning provides a higher-level and longer-term vision. It helps prepare the team for events that are expected to occur beyond the current Sprint and are identified as potential project risks. It also allows you to track progress over a longer term than the current Sprint.

The ninety-day wave rolls through the project schedule, which is updated regularly (weekly or every two weeks) to encompass the period from today to the next ninety days. See figure 19 for a representation of how it works.

You can use a shorter or longer period of days, as the demands of your project dictate. If many things change quickly, use a shorter timeframe. I suggest aligning it with a number of Sprints — three to four might be a better wave period. If little changes in a ninety-day timeframe, then perhaps extend the period to half a year.

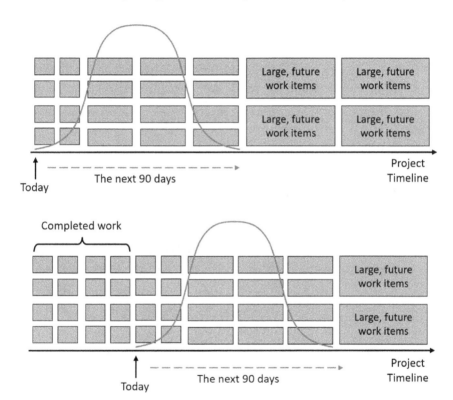

Figure 19: Rolling Wave Planning concept

Quarterly planning

One quarter of a year is often used to represent a planned increment of a large project, or group of projects, so scheduling and dependency management can be better managed across the group.

A planned quarter is different to Rolling Wave Planning because the plan is not constantly updated to represent the next ninety days. Instead, it represents a fixed period of the calendar year.

Three months (one quarter) of the year equals approximately six iterations of two-week Sprints. Quarterly planning is worth considering for large, complex, or multi-team projects, where the relevant teams, stakeholders, and customers gather and collaborate to form a high-level plan. In that process, they set out achievable goals, then break down the work, identify the team's capacity, and build a preliminary plan for the quarter.

As your organisation or stakeholders move away from time-bound project-based delivery, it is useful to have timeboxes of this size to plan larger projects or programs of work.

Imposing longer timeboxes helps to set and manage expectations for longer-term delivery schedules. Knowing what goal, issue, or dependency is coming up soon allows you and the team to do some preparation. It can be the difference between facing a blocker and not.

If you create a **longer-term plan** and allow it to change then you still meet the principle of *Responding to change over following a plan.*

This multi-Sprint planning does not match with Scrum. That's because Scrum takes the feedback from each Sprint to form the plan for the next one. Planning this far ahead potentially ignores the feedback the team will receive during Sprint Review. However, this planning can still be beneficial for identifying upcoming issues that are unavoidable and can't be delayed. The plan will provide you and the team with sufficient time to prepare. If you create this kind of plan and allow it to change from Sprint to Sprint, you are still applying Agile delivery. You are *responding to change instead of following a plan.*

Guessing the capacity of any future Sprint is the equivalent of making an assumption. The assumption is that the team's future Velocity resembles its most recent and that things won't change. The team can adapt the capacity of each Sprint to account for known impacts such as public holidays, annual leave, meetings, etc.

The diagram in figure 20 represents six sequential Sprints and allows a team to plan out work ahead of time by anticipating what they will work on in future Sprints.

Sticky notes represent a goal for each Sprint. It might be possible for your team to ascertain which Sprint Goal is achievable and would be most valuable. The other sticky notes below the line can represent either User Stories from the Product Backlog or Features that the team is working on. The idea is to represent the work to discuss and track it for a higher-level understanding of the project's progress and possible impediments.

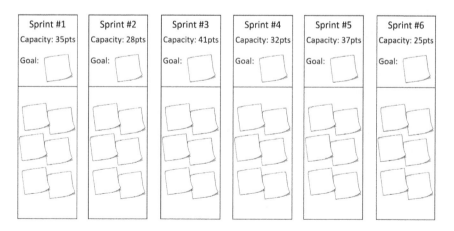

Figure 20: A quarterly plan made up of six Sprints

Planning horizons and product roadmaps

If you are working in a more mature Agile environment, you are likely delivering Features rather than Projects. You might also be delivering upon product goals rather than pre-defined scope. Building a roadmap with horizons is an excellent way to move away from timeline-based reporting and replace it with something meaningful.

The horizons help define the order of the focus areas and show what is being worked on now. They also indicate what is planned as the next focus. This format acknowledges the likelihood that plans will change rapidly. It helps you communicate with stakeholders that things will change, but you will still follow a planned approach.

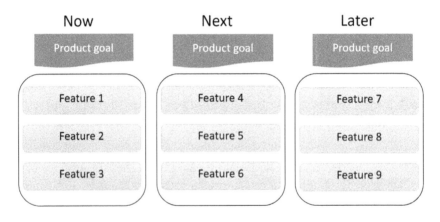

Figure 21: Simplified roadmap showing three horizons of planning

Your stakeholders can see product goals associated with each time horizon and know the next planned goal. The concept of Now/Next/ Later was introduced by Janna Bastow.[19]

Scrum of Scrums

If you are familiar with the daily Scrum, you will know its purpose is to 'inspect progress toward the Sprint Goal and adapt the Sprint Backlog as necessary, adjusting the upcoming planned work.'[20]

Scrum of Scrums lets you track and manage dependencies between teams.

You might consider holding a regular Scrum of Scrums when working on a multi-team project. The purpose is for delivery leaders to come together to discuss progress and impediments that either may impact other teams or that they need help to resolve. They can adapt their plan and Product Backlog as required, with the help of their Product Owners.

A multi-Sprint planning board or ninety-day wave plan are useful to coordinate efforts between teams and projects for things that require longer-term planning and preparation.

You can visualise and manage the dependencies between teams and track and manage the progress of larger deliverables that span multiple Sprints, such as larger Features and increments. Reminders on future Sprints help you keep on top of things that need to happen at certain points in the future, such as dependency management or release management.

Planning day

You might also choose to run a planning day if one of the following situations occurs:

- There is a large change either in stakeholders, project scope, ways of working, the make-up of the team, etc.
- You feel the project is getting off track or you can't see progress.
- There is a need for better coordination or dependency management between teams.

A planning day should include many of the same people as the original Discovery workshops if you believe the result will significantly change the project plan or schedule. Otherwise, only include those who are necessary, with representation from all the teams that depend on each other. The planned period aligns with a quarter or the next ninety days — not the entire project or longer durations.

Planning days should be a natural part of quarterly planning cycles, so they require regular scheduling and preparation.

In your session, aim to produce a goal for the planned interval, then form a high-level plan to achieve that goal. This might work at the Feature, Epic, or Story level, depending on how much detail you and your stakeholders need. Note that the more detail you go into (and the lower the level of planning), the greater the likelihood that the plan will change as you progress through delivery. This is expected because the plan changes as the team learns new things from the customer.

Make use of every element in this book to build a viable plan, and confirm it with your stakeholders and team. Use the capacity of each Sprint to set a constraint for what work can be planned into the Sprint. Get your stakeholders to agree on the priority, given the goal and limitations of time and capacity.

This is a prime opportunity to set and manage stakeholder expectations. Set aside Sprint capacity to make room for your team's learning activities, continuous improvement, scheduled meetings, holiday leave and public holidays. Show your stakeholders that it is unrealistic to expect your team to be working on the project all the time. They have other demands and expectations to fulfil.

You can plan Sprints with two or more teams when they have dependencies to complete Goals and release software. Illustrate the dependencies on the planning board using interconnecting lines and add other elements, such as when a risk is expected to be realised.

Add anything to the board that helps everyone anticipate important moments that need to be prepared for, any risks or dependencies that will become realised, a change to an environment, an expected code merge or systems integration. Include anything that requires work from the team that may not be captured in the product backlog and is time-sensitive. Ask your team what they would like to know in advance and what they would like to have added to the board.

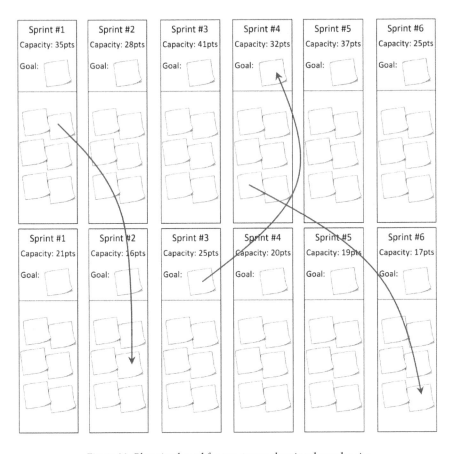

Figure 22: Planning board for two teams showing dependencies

Figure 22 shows an imagined planning board for two teams that depend on each other and want to plan out the next six Sprints to better coordinate and manage their work. The board shows dependencies between work items as arrows connecting sticky notes. This process allows you to monitor essential items, and your team to make allowances in Sprints to manage them.

CHAPTER EIGHT

Running Delivery

The day-to-day running of delivery mostly involves removing blockers for the team and ensuring they are supported to work well. Attending your team's regular Agile ceremonies is a chance to observe and learn what challenges they are experiencing and which they need your help with. The Daily Scrum is the best and most frequent opportunity to do this.

Resolving blockers

Monitor the flow and progress of work items using whatever workflow tool your team uses. You can identify work items that are getting blocked or delayed, question the causes, and then work with your team to remediate the blockage.

Agile has a concept called Swarming where if an individual is getting blocked and struggling to resolve a work item, the team members work together to find a solution.

Swarming is a technique for your team to rapidly resolve impediments.

The advantage of Swarming is that the team can protect the Sprint Goal and maintain progress towards the larger Product Goal.

The team can more effectively complete their work with your help in clearing impediments.

You can support this by tracking progress, identifying upcoming impediments and addressing them before they become a blocker for the team. It is a proactive approach to delivery — rather than reactive.

The value that you add to the team is to help them stay in the flow of delivering work items. Your goal is to limit distractions and impacts that may disrupt team members. Common disruptions include requests for information or assistance with things that do not immediately relate to the current project or Sprint Goal.

Sometimes those disruptions can be delayed or deferred because they are not time-critical or important. It's valuable for you to assess their significance. If you allow the team to be disrupted, then time it with a natural break in their work, which minimises the impact.

Reporting

One of the common disruptions for a team is a request for a status update or a progress report. If it concerns something non-critical, delay or answer it yourself. You can clarify what specific information is needed and ask the team at the right time.

It is better for you to manage regular reporting if that's what your management team or stakeholders seek. You can control the content, the frequency, and when to ask your team for information.

Note that Agile principles state clearly that *working software is the primary measure of progress.* Sometimes stakeholders need to be reminded of that when they ask for a comprehensive progress report. That means when the team members conduct their review at the end of every Sprint, they are demonstrating progress by presenting the latest version of the working software. It doesn't always satisfy all management and stakeholders, so further reporting is sometimes necessary.

Reporting can be disruptive to the team, so take control and provide reporting when it suits you and the team.

Try to take ownership of reporting by asking your managers and stakeholders what information they require and why. You can then present simple, informative reports that answer their needs and limit the impact on the team.

Reporting is a critical skill that builds and maintains stakeholder trust. When things go badly or unexpectedly, reporting can manage stakeholder expectations — in advance of a bad situation and while you resolve it. While stakeholders may not be close to you, your delivery team, and your collective situation, they are interested in the project's outcome. You are responsible for that outcome, so when things go wrong, you will need to have ready answers for what happened and what you are doing about it.

Reporting needs

The following list encompasses observed reporting needs from stakeholders I have worked with. Start here to confirm what is important to your stakeholders. You want to limit the amount of reporting because all reporting has an overhead to produce, and not all reporting is needed or relevant.

Potential reporting topics include:

How is the delivery team performing (in terms of completing the work efficiently)?
Is the team performing to expectation for a capable delivery team, or does something need to be improved?
If improvements are necessary, what is being done about it?
What problems are being encountered with delivery, and what solutions are being applied?
What changes are happening in the project or the team (scope, team members, role changes, etc.)?
What effects are these changes having?
What are the flow-on effects of these changes? Are future deliverables at risk?
What is the reason for scope changes and costs and time increasing?
Is the delivery team clear on what problem they are solving (the goal they are working towards)?
What are they currently working on to achieve the goal or solve the problem?
What is the current priority? What is the next priority? Why?
What is the quality of the work? Is it improving or worsening?
What do our customers and users think of the software?
What value has been delivered to our customers and users? How are we measuring that?
How are we tracking against business objectives that this project contributes towards?

What functionality (scope) has been cut or added to the project?
What decision do you need stakeholders to make? What are the options? What are the pros and cons of each option? What is the context of the decision? What is the impact of the decision?
What are the expected dates for deliverables? What does the roadmap look like?
How are our software systems performing (uptime, response rate, error rate, number of outages, etc.)?
How quickly are production incidents being resolved?
How many critical incidents are occurring?

It is worthwhile creating a simplified representation of the information your stakeholders need so they can gain an understanding from quickly looking at a report. They then only engage with you for clarification. If your stakeholders have all the information required, any regular meeting or forum is rapidly completed and less disruptive.

Brevity is essential in reporting — more information means more potential questions from your stakeholders, more work for you and more disruptions for your team. Only report that which is necessary.

Progress tracking and forecasting

As explained earlier, you can demonstrate progress using forecasting methods that help managers and stakeholders understand the current situation and the likely completion dates of work items. You might need to teach your stakeholders about Agile concepts, forecast-based reporting, changing scope, prioritisation and scope management.

> **Progress reporting** is your way of managing your stakeholders' expectations to free you and the team to work uninterrupted.

Progress tracking and reporting is your way of managing your stakeholders' expectations and keeping them satisfied that the team is completing work and meeting planned schedules.

An important call-out here is that there are two main approaches to forecasting the remaining work in the project. One is to estimate everything upfront, and the other is to estimate the work only when it is elaborated and prepared for development.

The first approach is more like Waterfall, where an entire backlog has been prepared and estimated. That might give your stakeholders more confidence in your team's progress because they can see it against a reasonably known and well-understood scope of work. However, it might also give them a false sense of confidence and become an issue when the scope of work keeps changing or when low-value scope items aren't completed by the project deadline because feedback increased the scope and took priority.

The second approach is to represent the scope of work as constantly increasing based on each new Sprint, with the items being estimated just in time. However, this might concern your stakeholders because they cannot see the end. The scope of work appears ever-increasing, and progress barely keeps up, meaning it seems that the project will never end.

An intermediate solution is to estimate each of the Features or Epics and track the progress of completed work against these preliminary estimates. This can be a practical step to help your stakeholders move away from traditional Waterfall progress reporting toward

Agile delivery. It enables them to see progress against the scope of work. It also allows estimates to change as Features and Epics are broken down into User Stories, and those User Stories are estimated individually.

A third method of progress tracking is the more traditional Gantt Chart, which lists all the work items that need to be completed in sequence, showing each item's order, duration, and dependency. The Gantt Chart is typically used in Waterfall projects where the list is known in advance and doesn't usually change. That doesn't suit Agile software delivery as the requirements are not expected to be known in advance and can change throughout the project.

Still, some tools emulate a Gantt Chart for use with Agile projects, and I will discuss them in the section on Planning in Jira.

Misinterpretation of progress reporting

In traditional organisations, a hierarchical structure represents how progress reporting is delivered to senior staff members.

There is an imagined line somewhere in that hierarchy. Below that line, people are familiar with Agile concepts and terminology and can speak and plan and report progress in these terms without explaining themselves. Agile uses language that is intentionally dissimilar to traditional project management.

There are almost always people above the line who are unfamiliar with Agile concepts. You cannot use Agile terminology to report to them because they don't understand it. Often they will ask for progress to be explained in a manner that they can understand.

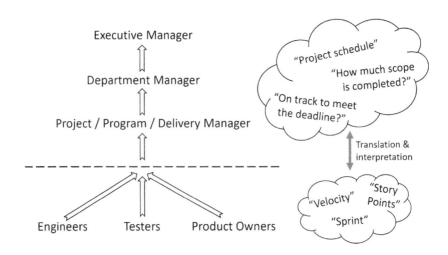

Figure 23: Translation between layers of hierarchy

Usually, someone in the hierarchy translates the delivery progress into something that the people above the line can understand. The problem with this is that it often obscures what is happening below the line. The person translating might misrepresent the progress or results — which is just as harmful to senior stakeholders.

Translating Agile concepts for senior stakeholders can obfuscate the reality, and it's important that you are transparent with them.

Transparency is at the heart of Agile, which means being careful to openly and honestly present the situation in a manner that people comprehend. You must ensure your senior stakeholders understand your progress and status reports. As author Simon Sinek wrote, 'Transparency doesn't mean sharing every detail. Transparency means providing the context for the decisions we make.'[21]

In figure 23, a dotted line runs through the hierarchical structure, separating those who understand Agile concepts and terminology from those who need it translated. The line might be higher (for example, above the project manager level), and the structure might be different, but the model is helpful in understanding where there can be miscommunication.

Senior stakeholders often want the ability to track the progress of work against an expected deadline. Consider any deadline flexible as new information is learned during the project.

Be very careful in your reporting to ensure that your senior stakeholders understand the progress, the challenges, the impediments and the impacts on your project. But do so in a way that they can consume the information and take action if required.

That might mean that you need to explain Agile concepts to bring them closer to the language that you and your team use. It might mean that you show them how to translate your reports into something they understand. Or it might simply mean that you need to use concepts that they are more familiar with. They should understand concepts like forecast modelling (which is covered in Velocity-based forecasting) as it will help them appreciate that things can change throughout the project.

You can create a metaphor to help them understand the concepts and show possible scenarios and outcomes. A good metaphor for Agile delivery is a driving directions app that provides an upfront estimate of when you can expect to arrive, based on everything the app knows about traffic congestion, speed limits, traffic lights, etc. The app updates its forecast of your arrival time as it learns new information while you are driving. If your path is impeded by heightened traffic or a road emergency, it communicates a delayed arrival time.

Resolving impediments

The ability to resolve impediments for your team is one of the most valuable contributions you can make toward project success. It usually requires calling upon other people for assistance which means you need to build your network within and outside the organisation. Sometimes you need help from people outside your company who have experience resolving a particular type of issue.

Meeting with your team and being constantly available makes it easier to resolve impediments as they occur. Make it easy for the team to contact you if you are not co-located.

It is good to look for themes and repetition in impediments, and you might consider recording them somewhere for this purpose. If there is consistency or repetition, use the Sprint Retrospective to look at ways of preventing or minimising them in the future.

Remote working and collaboration

Remote working can present particular challenges for the team. The benefits of being co-located are well known, which is why Agile promotes cross-functional, co-located teams. If your team cannot work this way, you need to provide them with methods and tools that closely simulate that environment.

The graph in figure 24 represents the effectiveness of various communication formats, with face-to-face at a whiteboard being the best possible format. Instant Messenger tools like Slack are the modern equivalent of email.

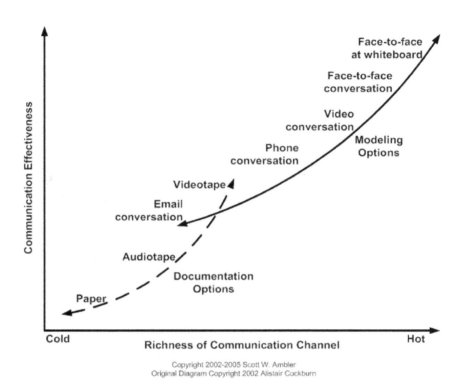

Copyright 2002-2005 Scott W. Ambler
Original Diagram Copyright 2002 Alistair Cockburn

Figure 24: Communication format effectiveness ©2002-

2005 S. W. Ambler. Original ©2002 A. Cockburn.

If the team cannot be co-located, you want to provide the next best thing — video conversation.

Given that whiteboard conversations are the richest and most effective, it is desirable to emulate a whiteboard conversation in a remote working environment. Online tools like Miro (https://miro.com) provide a very close digital copy of the physical whiteboard and sticky notes. I have seen Miro used extensively and successfully by teams working remotely for all manner of planning, analysis, discussion, problem-solving and solutioning.

Ways of working

Your team should discuss and agree on how they will operate and work together during the project. There are many factors to consider here, especially if they work remotely. Team cohesion is critical to successful project delivery, so you want the team to sort through options and challenges before they become issues.

Remote:AF (https://www.remoteaf.co) provides some excellent recommendations, templates and guides that can help your team agree on how to work remotely together.

Planning in Jira

It is worthwhile having a hierarchical view of the backlog and a timeline view of the work schedule. If you work in Jira (https://www.atlassian.com/software/jira), a product called Advanced Roadmaps can represent both the hierarchy and the timeline. It appears similar to a Gantt chart, so it should be easy to use and understand if you are familiar with that.

Advanced Roadmaps gives you the ability to plan out timelines for work items.

Advanced Roadmaps for Jira allows you to roll up estimates to a higher level. For example, if your project comprises Epics and User Stories, then estimates can be combined into a single number that represents all those items at the project level. It allows you to plan out timelines for work items by assigning target start and end dates, so you can see if there are scheduling clashes or dependency issues.

Advanced Roadmaps also provides progress tracking by calculating the number of completed work items (or Story Points) against all items in the project. This can save a great deal of effort with progress reporting, and give a real-time view of the scope and progress of the project. As new work items are added to the project in Jira, they appear in Advanced Roadmaps, meaning you get to see scope changes as they occur. It assists managers further up the hierarchy where miscommunication can happen because it resembles a Gantt chart but draws upon real data from the product backlog.

Finally, Advanced Roadmaps allows you to do scenario planning to experiment with different schedules and ways of managing dependencies and work items.

Use this tool to help your stakeholders move from a Waterfall to an Agile mindset, as they can see the work progress in ways they understand. They can see how the backlog adapts through regular inspection, customer feedback and re-prioritisation of work.

The following image is a basic example of Advanced Roadmaps. The layout shows the backlog and a timeline representing when it is expected to be worked on and completed.

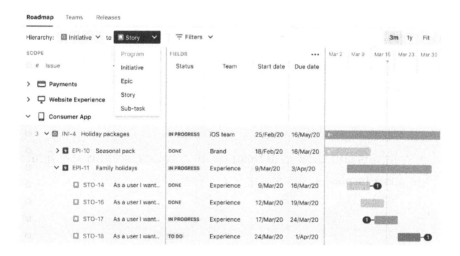

Figure 25: Advanced Roadmaps for Jira

The left column lists Jira backlog items according to their hierarchical structure. You can choose the level of depth, starting from Project (or Initiative) down to User Story or even sub-task. Figure 25 shows a drop-down list representing the hierarchical structure and the level of depth to display.

The next column contains typical project fields; progress status, team allocated, start date, end date (or due date).

The status column shows the status of work items taken from the Jira workflow status options.

You can allocate the target start and end dates for work items or let an automated scheduler work it out for you.

Advanced Roadmaps can also show a visual progress bar of a work item or group of work items, using shading to represent the percentage of completed work items. This progress figure is based on Story Points or the number of work items. The progress bar rolls up the progress of all items listed under each hierarchy level — excellent for communicating progress to your team and stakeholders.

The right-hand side represents a timeline that shows when a work item is anticipated to start and end. A bubble at the start or end shows where there is a dependency between line items. This section resembles a Gantt chart, translating progress for senior managers and stakeholders.

The columns and their order can be customised, so only use figure 25 as an example.

Customer feedback

Your team should be reviewing working software with the customer and receiving feedback that becomes additional work items in the product backlog for the Product Owner to prioritise.

It is not always possible to have access to a customer or end user during every Sprint. However, real customer feedback is essential to building quality software products, and there are several ways to get this.

You might choose to hold customer interviews at certain milestones in the project where they can provide the most valuable feedback. Alternatively, you might find a proxy who best understands the customers' needs and behaviours and can provide you with the same level of feedback as a real customer.

Another option is to ask an agency to conduct research and experiments that test your software with real customers and provide you with the results. Time and Motion studies can help you understand how easily and rapidly users can complete tasks and activities with your software.

The point here is that there are different ways to receive feedback on your software. Your team should have direct access to the customer to receive feedback, but it is worth exploring alternative options if they cannot.

The Product Owner should be present to witness the customer's experience and feedback and translate it into new Product Backlog Items. They should then prioritise those new items against other items in the backlog.

Adapting the backlog

Including customer feedback in the Product Backlog has the effect of increasing the scope of work. Low value items may not be completed if the delivery timeline is fixed and new backlog items are prioritised ahead of them. This may not be an issue unless some users or stakeholders expect those low priority items to be completed.

It will result in one of two things. The timeline and estimated budget will need to increase to accommodate the new scope (unless you have made allowances for variations), or there will be agreement that some low priority backlog items won't be completed.

You may need help from the users and stakeholders who attended Discovery to make this trade-off decision. However, doing so can be time-consuming and unproductive. In a perfect world, your Product Owner is entrusted to prioritise the backlog of work and make trade-off decisions that allow the schedule to be met (or over-run). Empowering the Product Owner is key to making these decisions run smoothly.

Things to watch out for

Unplanned work

One of the most significant factors impacting your project's delivery schedule is unplanned work. It can take many forms but is generally caused by people asking your team members to work on something that isn't part of the Sprint backlog. Requests come from outside of the team, from other team members ('Can you just do this thing for me?'), or even from a team member deciding that something is more important than the currently planned work.

Unplanned work can also be caused by feedback on incomplete work during development when presented to a Product Owner or user for clarity, confirmation or acceptance.

Unplanned work can cause your project to run much longer than originally estimated or planned.

While working on a User Story, the team member might receive feedback that is not part of the original acceptance criteria but is expected to be added or adapted. This is a common way for User Stories to increase in scope, impacting estimation, planning and the ability to release the next increment of working software at the end of the Sprint. Additional requirements should be added as new Product Backlog Items and then prioritised against all other backlog items.

The other source of unplanned work can be from the Product Owner, who may decide that they have something more important than the current Sprint backlog items and ask a team member to change what they're working on and replace items in the current Sprint. That may be acceptable if the team agrees that it's necessary and okay.

In figure 26, you can see that unplanned work enters the Sprint and consumes the capacity of the team needed to complete the Sprint backlog items. The effect is that the planned work doesn't get completed, which may mean the Sprint Goal is not achieved, and the team cannot review the completed increment at the end of the Sprint.

The potential long-term effect is that the planned work requires significantly more time to complete than initially predicted, casting doubt on the team's estimates and ability to deliver.

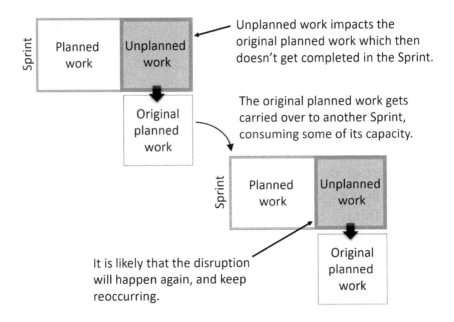

Figure 26: The impact of unplanned work on your project

You can take some actions to be aware of this situation, beginning with monitoring the team's Velocity and throughput. Any noticeable or consistent drop is an indication that unplanned work is occurring.

Monitor the items in the Sprint plan and look at which Product Backlog Items are committed to at the start and which are completed at the end. If the committed stories and completed stories are reasonably different, then it is likely that unplanned work has impacted the Sprint. I'll cover this in more detail in the next section on Incomplete Sprints.

Sometimes there are legitimate reasons why unplanned work needs to occur; something urgent comes up, or the team realises that they will be unable to complete a Sprint backlog item and work with the Product Owner to replace it in the current Sprint. When this occurs continually, it suggests the team is facing deeper issues, and you need to investigate and remediate the problem.

Splitting the capacity of a Sprint to allow for unplanned work can reduce the impact of unplanned work.

If disruption from defects in production or requests from people outside your team are constantly a problem, you may apply constraints on their impact on your team. Discuss and agree to allocate capacity within each Sprint to work on unplanned items. This will need the agreement of your stakeholders and sponsor, as it will have impact on the delivery schedule.

For example, you might decide that a maximum of twenty per cent of the capacity of each Sprint can be allocated to unplanned work. The remainder is for planned work that contributes to meeting the Sprint Goal and completing the project.

Incomplete Sprints

Keep watch for incomplete Sprints. These are observable with burndown charts. If the team is not getting through the backlog of work each Sprint, they may be experiencing problems. When a team is not mature with Scrum, they can fall into bad habits like constantly carrying a User Story from one Sprint to the next.

Figure 27 shows an example of a burndown chart where the team could not complete the committed User Stories within the Sprint. The top line represents the outstanding work, measured in Story Points. The Sprint started with 72 Story Points and ended with around 68, meaning little of the planned work was completed. The bottom line represents an ideal trend line showing continuous completion of work throughout the Sprint.

The fact that the top line goes higher during the Sprint is likely explained by new work introduced. Otherwise, the existing work was re-estimated during the Sprint and was more effort than initially anticipated. Both explanations are good reasons to examine what needs improving with Sprint planning and estimation.

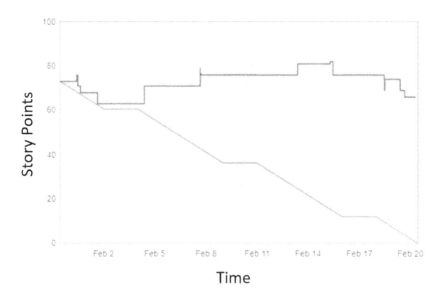

Figure 27: A burndown chart for an incomplete Sprint

Incomplete Sprints are problematic for two reasons. The first is that the team cannot present the updated software to customers for review and feedback. The second is that it impacts their ability to predict the capacity of a Sprint, meaning their estimates are poor and planning is inadequate. This increases the likelihood that any proposed end date has been incorrectly estimated and is unreliable.

The explanations for this vary. It could be that the team cannot break down User Stories sufficiently to complete them within a

Sprint timebox. In this case, it's worth taking them through training on how to break down User Stories. Too many interruptions during each Sprint may delay the User Stories they are working on. Investigate the disruptions and see how to prevent them or manage them better. Unplanned work brought into the Sprint can also cause difficulties.

Poor estimation can be caused by multiple reasons, and it's important to understand the cause.

If the team is not very good at estimating the amount of work they can complete in one Sprint, you'll need to present this data to help them improve their estimation and planning.

One final reason for an incomplete Sprint is that the customer or Product Owner changes the scope of User Stories once they have been started. Sometimes, during story acceptance, customers or Product Owners think of other things that they would like the software to do, so they ask the team to change the definition of the story to incorporate these new requirements. The story takes longer to complete, and the team appears to have mis-estimated it. Don't allow this to happen unless it is evident that the Sprint Goal can only be achieved if the story definition is changed. At that point, change the estimate to reflect the additional effort involved.

Encouraging customers and Product Owners to provide feedback and additional requirement requests during the Sprint Review will result in additional Product Backlog Items, which can then be prioritised into other Sprints. This is the best way to manage the scope and new requirements in an Agile project.

An exception to these reasons for incomplete Sprints is if the team consciously commits to more work than they typically can complete, to increase their capacity. Teams sometimes do this once they have made improvements — bringing additional work items into the Sprint as 'stretch items'. As teams become more efficient and effective, they can take on more work, which is an obvious way to increase capacity. If they don't complete those stretch items, it doesn't matter because they were in addition to the planned work. But if they can, it's a sign that they have increased efficiency.

Compare how many Story Points were *committed* to at the start of the Sprint with how many were *completed*. This will provide a simple way to gauge the maturity of your team's estimation and planning ability. A mature team will have low variance, as in figure 28.

Do not expect the team to complete all the Sprint backlog items every time. The team needs to be able to innovate solutions, which means they require some flexibility in what work they finish during the Sprint. Sometimes the result of innovation and learning is that work takes longer than anticipated.

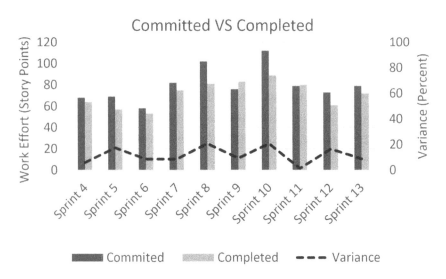

Figure 28: Track variance between committed and completed Story Points

Poor User Stories

At the heart of successful delivery is the quality of the User Stories that the team creates. Several issues might impact the delivery schedule if the stories are poorly written.

The first issue is that the User Stories require further refinement and clarification once an engineer has started them, wasting time and delaying testing and acceptance. It can also disrupt the Product Owner, customer or business stakeholder who needs to provide clarification. Ideally, User Stories should be fully elaborated and clarified before they are estimated and planned in Sprint Planning.

User Stories can carry over from one Sprint to the next. However, this impacts the team's ability to estimate and plan their Sprints and present working software at the end of every Sprint. It also affects the delivery schedule and your confidence in meeting an estimated deadline. Work closely with the team to understand why User Stories are carrying over and remediate the problem, so it doesn't continue to occur.

Another issue is that User Stories are often poorly estimated and take much longer than anticipated to complete. To identify this problem, track how many days a story stays in progress. If it's much longer than other stories of a similar estimate, identify the cause of the delay and remediate it.

User Stories can bounce between the engineer and the tester. This is usually because the engineer believes they have completed the story, while the tester considers it incomplete and needs more work. The problem is typically caused by User Stories that are ambiguous or missing important information.

> You can **improve story writing** by going through the INVEST practices with your team.

In most instances, you can solve these problems with your team by going through the INVEST practices of good story writing.

Another way to address these issues is to have a formal kick-off for every User Story. Here, the Engineer gathers the Tester, Product Owner and Business Analyst or whoever is intimately involved in completing the User Story, walks through their understanding and explains the plan to complete it.

This process allows for any last-minute corrections or adjustments and ensures that everyone in that group agrees on an aligned understanding. It minimises disruptions and saves on corrections and clarification throughout the completion of the User Story.

Team cohesion and conflict

Diversity of thinking requires alternative thinking and opinions, so your team members will have disagreements from time to time. These can be healthy and central to innovating solutions. The key is how they handle those disagreements and continue to work together. Sometimes they will need help, so here are some options.

The first and simplest method is to remind the team that it's okay to work through options and have disagreements. However, they need to be able to *disagree and commit* [22] at some point, meaning while they might differ, they still need to reach a conclusion and commit to it together. If they struggle with the concept, suggest they follow one decision as an experiment. And if that doesn't work out, revert to another option.

Another (more involved) method is for team members to learn and appreciate each other's personality profiles. It can help them understand each other's communication styles and preferred ways of working. Conflict within teams is often caused by ignoring people's preferences. For example, one person prefers face-to-face conversations, and another keeps making group decisions over email. The first person might feel they haven't had a fair opportunity because they were denied the opportunity to discuss the decision in person.

Get the two together, apart from everyone else, and facilitate a discussion that helps them appreciate each other's viewpoint and recognise their value and interests. This action can go a long way to defusing a heated situation.

Encourage your team to form a social contract that includes how they address conflict and disagreement as a team.

An excellent book is *The Five Dysfunctions of a Team* by Patrick Lencioni,[23] which discusses the typical problems a team faces and advises how to address those issues.

Managing for Happiness by Jurgen Appelo[24] is also excellent, with methods and tools to motivate your team.

Changes in stakeholders or management

The constraints, support and business goal you are working with are defined by the stakeholders and management team, either directly or indirectly. Changes in people or their roles and responsibilities can trigger a shift for your project. Sometimes this occurs without

Long-running projects increase the likelihood of stakeholder changes that impact your chance of success.

drawing much attention, but it can derail your project's success when you discover that things have changed.

It is worth speaking one-on-one with the new stakeholder to understand if they expect to make any changes that will impact your project. If there is a large amount of change, use the opportunity to re-confirm the agreements made during Discovery. That may require bringing some or all stakeholders and participants together to revisit the decisions and direction already made.

Note that the longer a project runs, the greater the chance that change will occur and impact your project. For this reason, it is beneficial to have shorter incremental releases because the work that has been completed and released already is (usually) unimpacted by these changes. You don't need to rework, delay or even cancel finished work.

Changes to the technical solution

A decision by the team, or someone outside it, that the technical solution design needs to change partway through the project can trigger a major change in the delivery schedule. Make sure you understand the impact before the team gets too firmly committed to the change. If it is significant, it might be worthwhile discussing it with stakeholders and management to confirm that they understand the importance and accept its impact.

If the change is not acceptable at this point in the project, ask the person who triggered it about the impact of delaying until later. This might enable the delivery team to continue their work and hold the change until a more convenient time.

Changes in engineering and testing practices

Occasionally, team members or people outside the team mandate that the engineering or testing practices need to change. The result is additional work and even rework, significantly impacting the delivery schedule. As with the technical solution change, take the opportunity to question the change and seek to delay it to prevent adverse impacts on the delivery schedule.

Changes in other constraints

Whenever a constraint is added or changed, it will likely impact the team and the delivery schedule. Often these changes occur quietly because someone has spoken directly to a team member and given instructions. Once you become aware of the situation, make sure you understand and even question or challenge it — especially if it significantly impacts the delivery schedule.

Getting agreement for significant changes

When seeking approval for making a significant change, outline the purpose, its value to stakeholders and/ or management, and any impact on the delivery schedule. The team will need to provide an updated estimate for delivery dates.

Resolving conflict when change is introduced is critical to your success.

Compiling this information and getting an agreement is vital for stakeholder management. If they are unaware, they only notice a missed delivery commitment when the project overruns its deadline.

Conflict may arise between the change instigator and your stakeholders, so gather them and ask:

- 'Is it important that we don't release further software changes without making this change?'
- 'Is there a more logical point where we can understand these changes before we begin applying them?'
- Is everyone in agreement that the delivery schedule will be delayed as a result of the change?'

It's important to understand the full scope of the change as if it applies to software that has already been tested, accepted and released, it can mean significant rework for any completed work.

Indecisiveness or overturning decisions

In organisations with a lot of bureaucracy, there might be conflict around important decisions that impact your project. The symptoms are that it takes a long time to make decisions, or decisions are constantly overturned — or both. These issues can block the team, add unexpected scope, or delay a project. That is where having a strong Product Owner is beneficial because they make most of the decisions that impact your project.

If you are experiencing issues with bureaucracy, a possible solution is to create a decision register, which is simply a place to record decisions. Once a decision is made, capture it in the register with the date, the agreed decision, and the person accountable for it. If anyone challenges the decision later, they need to convince the person who made it and any impacted stakeholders.

Future decisions can also be captured in the decision register. Assign a date by which the decision must be made or risk impacting the project. Document this thoroughly so your stakeholders know the decision, its impact, and the expected resolution date. Creating awareness can highlight that the decision is outside your (and your team's) ability to resolve. This also helps when assigning accountability for issues that impact your project but are outside your control.

A **decision register** is simply a place where you record decisions that have been made, or that need to be made.

Usually, there is a forum for making such decisions. It could be a risk management meeting or a steering committee meeting. If a group needs to make or confirm a decision, it is worthwhile providing background so each person can read and understand the trade-offs and impacts.

You might choose to document this and circulate it before the meeting so that attendees have time to consider it and are better prepared to discuss and decide within the forum.

Inflated estimates

Parkinson's Law tells us that work expands to fill the time available for its completion. That means that if teams are allocated more time than is required to complete a task (or User Story or Feature), they will often fill the remaining time with unnecessary work.

Allowing excessive estimates can mean inefficient use of available time. It suggests that you need to be aware of estimates that have been padded with a buffer or that are conservative. Consider challenging estimates if you believe the work can be done quicker or more efficiently. You can do so simply by asking probing questions when you are walking through them with your team:

- Why is the estimate higher than for similar work done in the past?

- Why is the estimate for this story higher than that one?

- Where is the effort (or complexity) in this User Story (or Epic) that makes the estimate that high? Can the effort (or complexity) be removed or changed?

- Is the high estimate on this User Story due to uncertainty? What can you do to reduce the uncertainty, such as a Spike? Do you need greater refinement (elaboration and clarity) to reduce the uncertainty?

- Is there another way to create a solution that reduces the estimate? What have you tried? Why did you choose that way?

- Have you consulted with other people to arrive at this estimate? Would you like more time to consult with people?

- How accurate do you feel this estimate is? What else can you do to increase the accuracy?

Resistance to meetings, workshops and Discovery

You might encounter complaints or resistance to holding these valuable meetings. Often it comes from influential stakeholders who believe they're a waste of time and people should spend more time sitting at their computers, 'doing work'.

Explain that the purpose of these workshops and meetings is to understand the customer's needs and design an optimal solution, which is important for delivering the software.

Challenge their resistance and their beliefs by asking, 'What's the cost of making a mistake when building software?' They almost certainly won't have an answer. There is no exact answer, but if you were asked for an estimate, remember it is almost always more costly to fix a mistake in code than in the Discovery and solution design phase. It shouldn't be hard to find evidence for your case.

If the organisation has had difficulties delivering projects in the past, then it's worthwhile explaining that you can't expect to improve on historical experiences without applying improvements. Use the evidence from historical Post-Implementation Reviews (if available) to show any mistakes made and how your method addresses them.

If they insist that it's a waste of time or money, remind them that you and your team are responsible for the timely delivery of the software, and as such, you choose how to minimise risks and mistakes.

Team collaboration is the primary way to resolve issues and challenges, and therefore to successfully deliver.

Explain that the way to resolve and prevent issues is to improve the communication bandwidth so that people are aligned on topics and decisions. The most common cause of problems is a lack of awareness or agreement, which is usually the result of people not understanding each other's views and opinions or having the same contextual awareness.

Project Acceptance and Formal Sign-off

There is often a specific step in the software delivery process in traditional Waterfall projects to formally approve the software before it is released. This step is called *User Acceptance Testing* (or UAT).

UAT is designed as a catch-all for things that have been missed or don't work correctly from the user's perspective. It represents a common cause of delay in project delivery for the following reasons:

- New stakeholders join the project who don't understand the original vision and requirements and bring their own requirements and expectations.

- Undocumented requirements have only just now been realised, which should have been captured during Discovery or delivery.

- Requirements have been misinterpreted or are ambiguous, and the person performing UAT disagrees that a condition has been met.

- UAT is performed in a different environment, and the software doesn't work properly in the new environment.

- UAT is performed with a different data set, and the software doesn't work correctly with this data set.

There can be a strong urge to raise issues because once UAT is completed, the project is generally signed off, and the budget is closed for any further changes. It is the last opportunity for stakeholders to make their changes.

UAT should not be needed in Agile projects because User Stories are accepted throughout the project by the Product Owner and possibly by the stakeholders and users. The team is incrementally completing the working software, including approvals, so final approval is unnecessary. If stakeholders or the Product Owner do not accept the acceptance step at the User Story level, you will need to formalise this as part of the Definition of Done.

The Definition of Done is like a contractual agreement with a set of criteria that states the steps required for a User Story (or a Feature, or a Release) to be accepted as complete. If each User Story, Feature or Release has met these criteria, it cannot be refuted that it has been done.

When following Agile principles, you won't be doing a big-bang release after spending a lot of time building functionality. Instead, you will incrementally release functionality as early and regularly as possible.

If your stakeholders insist on performing UAT to close out the project, restrict the testing to successfully completed User Stories. Facilitate the session with your team members present and have them operate the software to demonstrate that each User Story works according to the Acceptance Criteria.

Once each User Story has met the Definition of Done, and the Acceptance Criteria are satisfied, there should be no additional work for your team to satisfy UAT.

User Acceptance Testing should be unnecessary or merely a formality in an Agile software project.

If additional requirements arise out of UAT, then create backlog items, and explain that further work requires the agreement of the Product Owner and/ or change approval from the project stakeholders.

Retrospectives

The list of issues in this chapter is by no means complete, and you will constantly be observing challenges and impediments that the team is experiencing and looking for ways to resolve them. Use data as much as possible to reduce emotion and subjectivity. Look for repetitive issues and those that cause a considerable divergence from the schedule. Observe delays and blockages that impact the flow of work. Track these so you can prioritise the issues causing the greatest impact.

Afterword

The premise of this book is that you can ensure a better outcome for your project by conducting specific activities before and during delivery.

By now, you have an extensive list of skills to practice and develop, and these will assist you in becoming outstanding at delivery. Once you start successfully delivering for your stakeholders and your team, you will gain their trust and build their confidence in you.

You now have a solid understanding of how to combine Agile software delivery with longer-term planning, risk and issue management, stakeholder management, progress reporting and advanced estimation practices. You also understand the benefits and process of conducting Discovery before kicking off a project.

It may feel challenging to apply what you have learned. Every organisation comprises people who firmly hold to beliefs and ideas, and your new methods will test them. Work with each person to help them understand *why* you do things as you do. Talk about the benefits and show people what needs to change. Stay positive and focused. Concentrate on achieving successful outcomes, and explain how your skills will do that. Target early wins to demonstrate that your changes are the right path forward.

There are many artefacts and tools on my website: www.peterscheffer.com that can support your journey. While you're there, sign up for regular updates and useful information, and get in touch if you have a question I can help with.

What comes next?

This book has covered how to make Agile software delivery work in a project management environment by collaborating with your team and stakeholders. It hasn't covered how to change that environment to become more aligned with Agile values and principles.

You will find that it is not enough to just deliver projects. You also want to create a better environment for your team to work the way they want. They want greater autonomy, more say in the value delivered, better customer interactions, and the continuous iteration of solutions without time or budget constraints. They want to innovate to create memorable solutions that they are proud to build.

The improvements you make from your learnings here are localised to your team and perhaps some of your stakeholders. The next stage of transformational improvement is at the global level within your organisation. There, you will change the mindsets of managers and executives and ways of working for large groups of delivery teams. Your organisation benefits greatly from adopting Agile ways of working and allowing the software teams to deliver in their most optimal way.

That is the subject of my next book.

About the Author

Peter enjoys the art of creation, and software represents some of the most powerful and influential products that can change people's lives.

He started his career as a software engineer and soon learned that there was strong pressure to take shortcuts to meet deadlines within companies. When working in small teams, he would find himself responsible for consulting with stakeholders to understand their needs and discuss trade-offs. This led Peter to become a business analyst, where he influenced stakeholders and began to shape software to achieve better outcomes.

In Peter's experience, what was missing from Agile was the forethought needed to understand a problem and explore possible solution options fully. There was no design step where teams would sit down and work through solution designs. Again, there was the pressure to get started, with management often complaining, 'we're already behind schedule'.

It wasn't until Peter learned of Discovery and longer-term planning that using Agile for any reasonably large project made sense. The enjoyable aspect was the collaboration and empowerment that came from exploring the problem space, determining the best solution, and creating the plan to deliver it.

He has worked in large and small organisations, in government and the private sector, and built his own software projects. Peter has learned that empowered teams create better software, and organisations must adapt to allow them to do so.

When he is not empowering teams, Peter rides motorbikes, hikes in the wild, or backpacks in foreign countries.

You can connect with Peter here:

https://www.linkedin.com/in/peterscheffer/

peter@peterscheffer.com

www.peterscheffer.com

Glossary

Daily Scrum A team meeting to discuss progress and impediments.

Discovery A set of activities to broadly understand a body of work.

Feature A usable piece of functionality that allows users to complete a task or activity.

Iteration Work is delivered in Sprint cycles, each known as an Iteration.

Order of Magnitude (OOM) A very rough estimate that provides little detail.

PMO Project Management Office; a group of people responsible for overseeing project delivery.

Product Owner The person whose role is to ensure the team is doing valuable work.

Scrum Master The person who ensures the team is applying Scrum correctly.

Scrum of Scrums A meeting of team leads to discuss interdependencies, impediments and progress.

Spike	An activity that the team conducts to explore and/or research technical solutions.
Sprint	A specific timebox (period) allocated to complete work. A Sprint is often two weeks in duration.
Story Point	An abstract measurement of effort. A measure of estimation.
Swarming	A concept where the team works collectively to resolve blockers.
Throughput	A measure of how many work items are completed within a specific time frame, usually one Sprint.
User Story	A requirement given by a user or customer. Can also be given by stakeholders and delivery team members.
Velocity	The number of Story Points completed in a Sprint.

References

1. Atlassian. (2018). https://twitter.com/jira/status/968283998886682624

2. University of Cambridge. (2012). *Ounce of prevention, pound of cure.* https://www.cam.ac.uk/research/news/ounce-of-prevention-pound-of-cure

3. Blank, S. (2013). Why the Lean Start-Up Changes Everything. *Harvard Business Review.* https://hbr.org/2013/05/why-the-lean-start-up-changes-everything

4. Bloch, M. et. al. (2012). Delivering large-scale IT projects on time, on budget, and on value. *McKinsey.* https://www.mckinsey.com/business-functions/mckinsey-digital/our-insights/delivering-large-scale-it-projects-on-time-on-budget-and-on-value

5. Ibid.

6. Graham, P. (2004). *How to make wealth.* http://www.paulgraham.com/wealth.html

7. Ugarte, E. (2015). *Conquering Complexity.* Helmsman Institute.

8. Brown, D. W. (2011). In Praise of Bad Steve. *The Atlantic.* https://www.theatlantic.com/technology/archive/2011/10/in-praise-of-bad-steve/246242/

9. IDEO U. (2022). *What is Design Thinking?* https://www.ideou.com/blogs/inspiration/what-is-design-thinking

10. Wikipedia. (2021, October 22). *Five Whys.* https://en.wikipedia.org/wiki/Five_whys

11. Adzic, G. (2012). *Impact Mapping: Making a big impact with software products and projects.* Provoking Thoughts.

12. Riordan, C.M., & O'Brien, K. (2012). For Great Teamwork, Start with a Social Contract. *Harvard Business Review*. https://hbr.org/2012/04/to-ensure-great-teamwork-start

13. Wake, B. (2003). INVEST in Good Stories, and SMART Tasks. *XP123*. https://xp123.com/articles/invest-in-good-stories-and-smart-tasks/

14. Lawrence, R., & Green, P. The Humanizing Work Guide to Splitting User Stories. *Humanizing Work*. https://www.humanizingwork.com/the-humanizing-work-guide-to-splitting-user-stories/

15. Adzic, G. (2012). *Splitting user stories — the hamburger method*. https://gojko.net/2012/01/23/splitting-user-stories-the-hamburger-method/

16. Patton, J. (2014). *User Story Mapping: Discover the Whole Story, Build the Right Product*. O'Reilly.

17. Cohn, M. *Planning Poker*. Mountain Goat Software. https://www.mountaingoatsoftware.com/agile/planning-poker

18. Wikipedia. (2021). *Cone of Uncertainty*. https://en.wikipedia.org/wiki/Cone_of_Uncertainty

19. Bastow, J. (2019). *The Birth of the Modern Roadmap*. https://www.prodpad.com/blog/the-birth-of-the-modern-roadmap/

20. The 2020 Scrum Guide. https://scrumguides.org/

21. Sinek, S. (2022). https://twitter.com/simonsinek/status/1506697288818774019

22. Wikipedia. (2021). *Disagree and commit*. https://en.wikipedia.org/wiki/Disagree_and_commit

23. Lencioni, P. M. (2002). *The Five Dysfunctions of a Team: a leadership fable*. John Wiley & Sons.

24. Appelo, J. (2016). *Managing for Happiness*. John Wiley & Sons.

List of Figures

Index

www.ingramcontent.com/pod-product-compliance
Lightning Source LLC
Chambersburg PA
CBHW071120050326
40690CB00008B/1288